THE BANK OF NORTH DAKOTA: AN EXPERIMENT IN AGRARIAN BANKING

STUDIES IN HISTORY, ECONOMICS AND PUBLIC LAW

EDITED BY THE FACULTY OF POLITICAL SCIENCE
OF COLUMBIA UNIVERSITY

Volume CXIV] [Number 1

Whole Number 254

THE BANK OF NORTH DAKOTA: AN EXPERIMENT IN AGRARIAN BANKING

BY

ALVIN S. TOSTLEBE

AMS PRESS
NEW YORK

COLUMBIA UNIVERSITY
STUDIES IN THE
SOCIAL SCIENCES

254

This Series was formerly known as
Studies in History, Economics and Public Law.

Reprinted with the permission of Columbia University Press
From the edition of 1924, New York
First AMS EDITION published 1969
Manufactured in the United States of America

Library of Congress Catalogue Card Number: 74-82241

AMS PRESS, INC.
NEW YORK, N. Y. 10003

To

MY PARENTS

PREFACE

In 1919 the farmer legislature of North Dakota made provision for a bank which embodied many novel features. Coming as it did at a time when the American people were earnestly engaged in an attempt to solve the rural credits problem it bade fair to command a good deal of attention and perhaps exert no little influence on future legislation.

Unfortunately the Bank was scarcely organized before it became the central issue in an exceedingly acrimonious political battle. Thereafter the Bank became the subject of many written articles. But, as might be expected, most of them betray a pronounced political bias and many are filled with the most extravagant statements which describe the Bank either as a notable success or a colossal failure depending upon the political persuasion of the writer.

The author was greatly attracted to the task of investigating the Bank's history because it appeared that the results of the North Dakota experiment were about to be lost under a welter of politically inspired propaganda. Society at no time can well afford to lose the lessons of experience; least of all when it is wrestling with a definite problem upon which a current experiment would throw some light. Hence it seemed particularly desirable that a scientific investigation of the Bank of North Dakota be made by one sufficiently detached from the state as to insure an open and unprejudiced mind. At first many misgivings were entertained concerning the practicability of attempting the task in a place so far removed from the state as New York City. Then came the suggestion that such physical isolation might be an advantage to the investigator, since it would be easier for him to maintain an unbiased point of view. As the work proceeded the wisdom of the suggestion became manifest. No part of the work was more difficult than to keep the mind riveted to the ideal of impartial appraisal and interpretation of facts which could seldom be found free from partisan adornments.

A work of this kind is of little value if it is in any way warped by political bias. Hence the author has steadfastly striven to present the unvarnished truth as he was able to discover it from the material at hand. As might have been expected this course led to the necessity of recording some events which are not complimentary to the management of the Bank. But, as will later be pointed out in the text, its officers were working under the most adverse circumstances. Neither the Nonpartisans nor the Independents were able to withstand the political pressure under which they were compelled to labor. The wonder is that they were able to carry on as well as they did.

Since there is much to be praised and much to be condemned in the management of the Bank under both administrations it is difficult to see how this record and appraisal of the Bank's activities can be used by either political faction in North Dakota as a weapon against the other. On the other hand it is hoped that the facts and analysis here presented will prove helpful to the many earnest citizens, members of opposing political factions, who are seeking to improve the financial position of the North Dakota farmer.

The author is indebted to a number of individuals for material and information which they have generously afforded. In this connection should be mentioned President E. G. Quamme of the Federal Land Bank of St. Paul.

Secretary O. E. Dieson of the Minneapolis-Trust Joint Stock Land Bank; Dr. W. H. Steiner of the College of the City of New York; Hon. Thomas Hall, Secretary of State (N. D.); Mr. Lewis F. Crawford, Secretary of the Industrial Commission of North Dakota; and Bank of North Dakota officials of both administrations.

Professor E. R. A. Seligman, and Mr. J. H. Nelson of the New York *Journal of Commerce* have read the manuscript and have made valuable suggestions. Professor H. Parker Willis has given generously of his time to the reading and criticism of the manuscript at every stage of its development. The author wishes gratefully to acknowledge his indebtedness to him for invaluable suggestions and criticism.

ALVIN S. TOSTLEBE.

COLUMBIA UNIVERSITY, JANUARY, 1924.

CONTENTS

PAGE

APPENDIX A

APPENDIX B

APPENDIX C

INTRODUCTION

Agriculture has been a fundamental industry in America from the beginning. Nevertheless, until recently, certain of its aspects have received little study and consideration from public men. The United States possessed a magnificent territory the fertility of whose lands served to postpone the demands of the farmers for modern machinery to finance their operations and market their produce. But, after a while, the haphazard methods of business, which were effective enough when competition was not keen, became inadequate. The time has arrived in American agriculture when the farmer must conduct his operations according to business principles. This cannot be done unless he has commercial facilities appropriate to his requirements. In recent years there has been an insistent demand for new and adequate machinery with which to finance and market farm produce. Within the past decade this demand has been generously met with a vast amount of state and national legislation—some good, some bad and some indifferent.

Farming, like most other businesses, embraces three distinct operations: production, marketing and financing.

Production on the farm involves the growing and harvesting of crops, and the breeding and feeding of livestock. The crops may be the great staples as corn, wheat and cotton; they may be the fruits of orchard and vineyard; they may be the berries and vegetables of the truck farm. Livestock may be bred and fed for power, for dairy produce, for wool, for eggs or for the butcher's block. Whatever the farmer essays to raise he finds that successful production requires a specialized knowledge of soils, varieties of crops and of livestock, together with an understanding of their conservation and care.

However, in a new country where good land is accessible to all at a nominal price farmers seldom turn their attention to the strictly scientific aspects of their business. For this, two reasons may be given. The first is that competition for land, with its resultant high rents, is little in evidence. Consequently the farmer is not spurred into a careful consideration of how he can produce the most profitable crop upon a given plot of land. A comparatively sparse population and a country richly endowed by nature is a combination of fortuitous circumstances which has permitted American farmers to remain indifferent to the science of agriculture. The same is true of animal husbandry. Only in a new country can farmers survive the practice of feeding good grain to inferior stock.

The second reason why farmers in a new country fail to consider more carefully their production problems is that they look for their greatest money gain in the advance of land values which is almost certain to follow an increase in population. Normally they have not been disappointed. Hence, if they can make a living and enough extra to hold their farms, they will, with the passing of years, attain considerable wealth by reason of the growth of the unearned increment of land value. The growth of the unearned increment is almost entirely independent of their efforts. Thus another strong incentive to make farming a scientific business has been lacking.

Fortunately our Government anticipated the time when the size of our population would make haphazard production of foodstuffs impossible, and, with proper appreciation of the importance of exact knowledge of both plant and animal husbandry, established an excellent system of experiment stations modeled after similar European institutions. Moreover, it made generous provision for the founding of agricultural colleges. Thus encouraged, most of the states cooperated with the Federal Government. Not only did they aid in developing the agricultural colleges, but also in the important work of the experiment stations. More recently still, the practical results of the research obtained at the experiment stations and the scientific knowledge to be had at the colleges have been brought to the farm in many localities by the county agricultural agents; and the Federal Government is now assisting in disseminating scientific agricultural knowledge in many of the public high schools of the country.

The labors of these various public institutions together with those of the United States Department of Agriculture have been exceedingly fruitful. Plant and animal parasites and diseases have been successfully combated; soils have been analyzed and recommendations made for their use, preservation and improvement; new crops and new varieties of old crops have been developed to the great enhancement of the farmer's wealth. Livestock has also been improved, and breeding and feeding established on scientific bases. So great have been the results that it would be impossible for anyone to estimate, with even a pretense of accuracy, the vast amount of benefit that farmers have received from these public sources.

Likewise national, state and local governments have lent substantial assistance in securing adequate transportation facilities for the farmer. At first the national and state governments made grants of land to the railroads; counties and cities issued bonds to raise funds for the use of the transportation companies. But after 1870 the public's interest underwent an important change. The decade 1860-

70 had been one of great expansion of the railway net. Railway mileage grew from 30,626 to 52,922. With this great growth came an intense rivalry for traffic between competitive points. The result was that rates on such cities were materially cut, while at the same time rates on intermediate towns were maintained at the old level. This local discrimination greatly incensed the farmers and those who lived in smaller towns, for it appeared that the railways were unjustly favoring shippers in the large cities at the expense of the rural population. The consequence was that public aid largely ceased and public regulation began. During the seventies many of the middle-western and western states passed laws designed to remedy the evils of local discrimination. Most of the laws provided for a commission to determine maximum rates. However, a state could not regulate a railroad beyond its own borders. Early court decisions conceded that a state had power to regulate that part of interstate traffic which was carried on within its own borders. But in 1886 the Supreme Court decided that the several states had no right to regulate interstate commerce at all and that they must confine their regulation to intrastate traffic. This decision made Federal legislation imperative and in the following year Congress passed the Interstate Commerce Act.

The laws passed by the great agricultural states in the seventies are frequently referred to as the "granger laws." They represent an attempt on the part of the rural population to correct abuses from which they as a class were suffering at the hands of the railroads. Since 1887 Federal legislation has transcended in importance that of the states. Subsequently Congress has passed many important laws designed to regulate and improve the railroad service. But it must be confessed that the present condition of railway service is entirely satisfactory to no class, least of all to the farmers.

Passing to the problems associated with the marketing of farm products, it is to be observed that they too were long neglected. Recently, however, there has been a rapid development of legislation seeking to regulate market agencies and to improve marketing conditions. A number of states as well as the nation have participated. It is generally recognized that the solution of the farmer's marketing problem lies in the direction of cooperative agencies for the grading, handling and selling of his produce. No less than thirty-five states now have laws under which farmers may organize into cooperative associations, and Congress has passed laws removing certain obstacles to cooperative organization which have hitherto existed. Indirectly, therefore, both state and national governments have endeavored to aid in the solution of the farmer's marketing problem.

There has also been direct aid. A number of states and the Federal Government have passed laws designed to regulate market agencies in the terminal cities, and to standardize certain methods and practices. The great interest that the Federal Government is now taking in the problem is shown by the detailed study and attention given to it by the Bureau of Agricultural Economics in the United States Department of Agriculture. Not only does this Bureau constantly conduct definite investigations into the methods and costs of marketing the various farm products with a view to obtaining practical information which will assist farmers to more economical methods of marketing, but it has also been charged with the administration of important Federal laws; namely, the so-called Cotton Futures Act, the Grain Standards Act, the Standard Container Act and the Warehouse Act. Apparently the Federal Government now fully appreciates the nature of the problem and the painstaking effort necessary for a satisfactory solution.

But progress in both agricultural production and marketing depends upon and is limited by the extent to which the farmer has access to capital. Thus it proves that the heart of the economic problem of the farm is financial, and progress in every direction awaits the solution of the rural credits problem.

As the American farmer pushed westward to possess the fertile lands there abounding, he was constantly embarrassed because he lacked the necessary funds with which to purchase land and carry on his farming operations. The Federal Government sensed the difficulty as early as 1800 and for twenty years thereafter disposed of public lands on a credit system. This was but a partial solution of doubtful value, and for a generation or two before the Civil War it was left to the states to provide credit facilities. To meet the need many of the western and southern states made provision whereby banking institutions of the most perverted kind could be established. Thus the so-called "wild-cat" banks sprang up and flooded the country with bank notes of uncertain value. The severe business crisis of 1837 was a direct result of unwarranted expansion made possible by an undue extension of credit by these mushroom institutions. The chaotic condition in which they constantly kept the nation's currency was one of the two important reasons which prompted Congress to create the National Banking System in 1863.

The National Banking System did not make credit conditions any more satisfactory for the farmer. There was, indeed, no direct discrimination against him; although indirectly, and by reason of his peculiar situation and needs, the farmer was largely barred from sharing in the benefits of the new system. To begin with, the $50,000 minimum capital requirement made the general establishment of national banks in rural communities impossible. Few indeed were the farming districts that could raise so large a sum. Moreover, when the original act was thoroughly revised in 1864 a provision was inserted forbidding loans on real estate. Both of these provisions were probably born of the sad experience with "wild cat" banks whose insufficient capital and unwise farm loans resulted in ruin to many western farmers. They undoubtedly were sources of strength in the new system; nevertheless, they practically annihilated its usefulness to the farmer.

In this connection the ten per cent tax on state bank notes (1865) takes on a new significance. While this measure may have been a wise and necessary provision if the nation's currency was to be stabilized, yet it was the death-blow to many a state bank; and the state banks were then the chief source of rural credit. Thus the farmer really bore a heavy portion of the hardships incident to purging our currency of the redundant and spurious state bank notes.

For a number of years agriculture was extended in spite of the lack of any adequate financial support. Free lands were still to be had, and under the Homestead Law of 1862 less financial assistance was needed to obtain them than ever before. But the need for rural credit facilities was bound to be felt sooner or later and would come when the supply of free lands was exhausted. Thereafter, competition for farms would take on a new significance and farm prices would greatly advance. As time went on those prices would become of greater and greater importance. It would take more and more money to purchase and equip a farm, and the necessity of providing those who were engaged in farming with adequate credit facilities would become imminent.

Two tendencies of the past several decades may be noticed in practically every agricultural state. One is a great increase in farm mortgages; the other is an alarming increase in tenancy. The former may be offered as proof of the assertions in the preceding paragraph; the latter that we have lacked, at least until very recent years, proper rural credit facilities.

Beginning with 1900 the National Bank Act has been so amended as to make it useful to the farmers. In that year the minimum capital requirement for national banks was reduced to $25,000 for towns not exceeding 3000 inhabitants. This made possible their establishment in communities that theretofore could not provide the larger capital. Moreover in 1913 national banks were given legal authority to loan on real estate security in amounts not to exceed twenty-five per cent of their capital and surplus, or thirty per cent of their time deposits.

Besides authorizing national bank loans on real estate the Federal Reserve Act recognizes the longer period of production on farms than in other businesses, and, accordingly, permits federal reserve banks to rediscount nine months agricultural paper, whereas other paper may not be rediscounted unless it is within ninety days of maturity.

Following the passage of the Federal Reserve Act there has been great legislative activity on the part of Congress in behalf of rural credits. In 1916 the Federal Farm Loan Act was passed. It provided for twelve federal land banks and an indefinite number of joint-stock land banks. In 1921 Congress, by joint resolution, converted the War Finance Corporation into an agency primarily to finance the exportation of agricultural produce. Later in the year legal provision was made whereby loans could be made to dealers in agricultural products, including cooperative organizations, for the purpose of financing the carrying of such products until they could be exported or sold for export in an orderly manner. Such advances could be made up to July 1, 1922. In June 1922 Congress passed a law extending for one year the time in which the advances could be made, and in March 1923 extended the time to March 31, 1924.

Finally, in 1923 Congress passed legislation which further liberalized the federal reserve system in behalf of farmers, provided for twelve federal intermediate credit banks presumably to finance agricultural operations which consume more than nine months time, but are of too short duration to warrant the use of federal land bank funds, and made possible the organization of an indefinite number of national agricultural credit corporations. Thus within ten years Congress has established a complex system of banks designed to meet rural credit needs of every legitimate kind.

A number of states have aided the farmers to obtain loans on farm mortgages. Some, as Colorado, Indiana, Iowa and others, have made provision whereby certain school funds, or funds derived from the sale of public lands may be loaned on farm mortgages. Others, as Montana (1915) and South Dakota (1917) have created rural credit systems in which funds to be loaned on farm mortgages will be secured through the sale of state bonds. Still others, as Missouri (1915) and New York (1914) have created state land banks. But no state has yet attempted so novel and daring a scheme for financing the farmer as did North Dakota when in 1919 the Bank of North Dakota was created.

It is to be expected that the vast amount of banking machinery and other agencies for supplying rural credit created so hastily during the past decade will sooner or later manifest serious defects, and the banking laws will need careful amendment from time to time. A painstaking study of the structure and operation of the various agencies now on trial should disclose their respective weaknesses and merits. Public men whose responsibility it will be to recast some of the laws will do well to consider dispassionately the several institutions as they actually function in the field. In this way alone can progress toward an indefective rural credit system be rendered certain.

It is hoped that this monograph describing one of the interesting experiments now on trial may be useful in revealing both the merits and defects of the Bank of North Dakota as four years of operation have brought them to light. If it succeeds in this, the lessons drawn from its history may be of service to those who are earnestly endeavoring to improve the several state and national rural credit systems.

CHAPTER I

Agricultural Conditions in North Dakota

SOIL AND CLIMATE

North Dakota was organized as a state from a part of Dakota Territory and was admitted to the Union in 1889 Its boundaries were fixed so as to embrace an approximate land area of 70,183 square miles.[1] As to size, therefore, it is typical of the middle-western states. It has a variety of soils. The eastern part lies in the Great Red River Valley of the North while the western part of the state is much less fertile and doubtless never can become a rich farming country. The geographic location of North Dakota is such that it possesses a somewhat rigorous climate. On the Canadian border and far from any tempering body of water, its seasons are severe. Winters are long and cold. The growing season is short, but intense while it lasts. Precipitation is not heavy in any part of the state, not exceeding twenty inches a year in the more humid sections and falling well below eight inches during the summer months in almost the entire western half of the state.

POPULATION

North Dakota is a sparsely settled state. Census figures show that its population has grown during the last thirty years as follows: [2]

[1] *Fourteenth Census of the United States*, 1920 Bulletin, Population: North Dakota, p. 1.

[2] *Ibid.*

Year	*Population*
1890	190,983
1900	319,146
1910	577,056
1920	646,872

In 1920, therefore, the average number of inhabitants to the square mile was only 9.2. Needless to say this is mainly a rural population. In 1920 there were only three cities in the entire state that had as many as 10,000 inhabitants, and only twelve that boasted of 2,500 or more. In the three census years of 1900, 1910 and 1920 the following percentages of the total inhabitants were to be found in the various communities: [1]

	1920	*1910*	*1900*
Cities of 10,000 inhabitants or over	7.2	4.6	
Cities of 5,000 to 10,000 inhabitants	2.9	2.9	5.4
Cities of 2,500 to 5,000 inhabitants	3.5	3.4	1.9
Cities, towns and villages of less than 2,500	19.6	17.0	15.0
Other rural territory	66.8	72.0	77.7

This rural population is of a sturdy and enterprising type. They have come to North Dakota from the various older agricultural states and a large part of the population either came from Northern Europe or are the children of such immigrants. Scandinavia, Russia, Germany and other neighboring European countries have contributed to the rugged and industrious population of the state.

CROPS

According to estimates of the United States Department of Agriculture the acreage, yield and value of the various North Dakota field crops for 1920 were as follows: [2]

[1] *Fourteenth Census, op. cit.*, p. 2.

[2] *United States Department of Agriculture Yearbook*, 1920.

Crop	Acres	Bushels	Value
Corn	711,000	17,064,000	$12,286,000
Wheat	7,600,000	68,400,000	88,920,000
Oats	2,485,000	59,640,000	20,874,000
Barley	1,260,000	22,680,000	12,701,000
Rye	934,000	9,340,000	11,115,000
Potatoes	90,000	7,110,000	6,968,000
Flax	735,000	3,896,000	6,935,000
Tame Hay	715,000	894,000 (tons)	8,851,000
Wild Hay	2,052,000	2,052,000 (tons)	23,598,000
Total	16,582,000		$192,248,000

A surprisingly large amount of corn is raised. This is, however, a recent development. Twenty years ago only 23,824 acres yielding 381,184 bushels were reported, only a few types of corn being then adapted to North Dakota conditions.[1] In 1910 corn-production figures had grown to an acreage of 214,000 and a yield of 2,996,000 bushels.[2] Apparently the last decade has witnessed the really rapid growth of corn-raising in the state.

The climatic conditions account, in large measure, for the trend that agricultural development has taken. The farmer of two or three decades ago found the North Dakota climate too severe for growing the varieties of corn then developed. Clovers and grasses did well, but the pioneer farmer with his limited means was usually in no position to possess the cattle which might have turned these crops into good profit. Moreover the severity of the winters made a specially large outlay necessary for the proper sheltering of the stock. Consequently the cereals were turned to as the most profitable crop that could be produced. These and flax frequently proved to be very profitable on new breaking. The tendency was, then, to concentrate effort on the small grains, particularly wheat, for the raising of which North Dakota

[1] *United States Department of Agriculture Yearbook*, 1900.

[2] *Ibid.*, 1910.

has many special advantages. A combination of climatic and soil conditions make possible the production of the finest milling wheat that the world produces. The hard spring wheat, out of which the finest grades of flour are milled, constitutes the largest crop raised whether measured in number of acres, in yield, or in money return.[1] There is, therefore, every reason to believe that wheat will continue to be the main crop of the state.

DIVERSIFICATION OF FARMING

However, the future welfare of the state and of the spring wheat industry depends on the maintenance of the fertility of the soil. This is impossible under the system of cropping that the average farmer follows. The soil cannot endure successive crops of wheat or other small grains for many years, when they are sold off the ground and no fertility returned. Eventually, and the sooner the better for the state, farming must assume a diversified aspect. This will necessitate proper rotation of crops and above all the feeding of considerable portions of the crop to stock on the farms. Some progress has been made during the past decade. Especially to be noted is the increased number of cattle kept on farms. Here the decade witnessed an increase of over 117 per cent. The increase in the number of sheep was more moderate, being 23.8 per cent. However, this is not as great a gain as it appears, for we must bear in mind that the acreage in farms has also increased during the decade, and a fair measure of the increase must make allowance for this. When the number of acres per head of cattle in 1920 is compared with similar figures for 1910, the increase is only 70.8 per cent.[2] Figured in this way, sheep actu-

[1] *Fourteenth Census of the United States*, 1920 Bulletin, Agriculture: North Dakota, p. 9.

[2] *Ibid.*

ally suffered a decrease in numbers. All in all there is still much to be hoped for in the proper stocking of the North Dakota farms before the present method of "soil-mining" is checked. With respect to other criteria for measuring improvement of method in farming, little is available. An increase of 70.5 per cent for 1919 over 1909 is recorded paid to hired labor; but it is very doubtful if this figure means anything at all in the way of increase because of the vastly different wage scales current in 1909 and 1919. The expenditures on commercial fertilizer increased from $10,003 in 1909 to $119,782 in 1919. These figures are too small to be of much significance, except as they may reveal a definite tendency. Here also the apparent increase must not deceive us, the different price levels of 1909 and 1919 accounting for much of the increase. More encouraging are the amounts spent by North Dakota farmers for feed. In 1909 a little over $2,000,000 was spent for feed, while in 1919 well over $12,000,000—an increase of more than 518 per cent.[1] Of course, allowance for changes in the price level will greatly change this figure, but still there is, no doubt, a considerable actual increase.[2]

FARM IMPLEMENTS

Such figures as are available on implements and machinery are quoted in terms of dollars—a very unsatisfactory stand-

	Cattle	*Sheep*
1920	1 head per 27.1 acres	1 head per 121.1 acres
1910	1 head per 46.3 acres	1 head per 117.7 acres

[1] *Fourteenth Census, op. cit.*

[2] In 1919 the index numbers for various types of commercial feeds were as follows: Farm products 234; Straight feeds, e. g. bran, cottonseed meal, etc. 236; Ready mixed 220. Since the North Dakota farmer did not need to buy the farm products and further since he buys very little ready mixed feed, the index number for straight feeds is the significant one. Index numbers taken from *Report of the Federal Trade Commission on Commercial Feeds*, p. 192.

ard by which to make comparisons over a period of years. However, the figures may be submitted for what they are worth. In 1880 the average value of farm implements and machinery to the acre was 81 cents; in 1890, 87 cents; in 1900, 90 cents; in 1910, $1.54; and in 1920, $3.15. The constancy of these values through the four decades is striking, but it may be accounted for when the methods of farming are observed.[1] There is very little "elasticity of demand" for machinery in a state like North Dakota. As has been mentioned above, the seasons are short and intense. Plowing, seeding and harrowing must be accomplished under pressure of time; and the grain must be harvested in a few hurried days. Consequently the farmers of the eighties and nineties were compelled to invest in a stock of machinery which in size was practically sufficient to meet the needs of the farmers during the last two decades. Recent increases may be accounted for by the fact that the co-operatively owned threshing machine is becoming very popular and that the tractor is supplanting the draft horse to a considerable extent.

SIZE OF FARMS

With the introduction of these larger types of machinery has come an interesting development in the size of farms.[2] Whether all the land included in farms is taken or only the improved land, the trend is the same. As an example take the former. In 1880 the average farm acreage was 271.2.

[1] The Federal Trade Commission made a study of price conditions in the farm implement trade and found that prices had increased on an average of seventy-three per cent from 1914 to 1918. It is, therefore, fairly safe to conclude that by 1920 this increase had reached one hundred per cent. See *Report of the Federal Trade Commission on the Cause of High Prices of Farm Implements*, p. 77.

[2] Farm means all land directly farmed by one person managing and conducting farm operations either alone or with hired help.

Similar figures for each decade following, and including 1920 are respectively 277.4, 342.9, 382.3, and 466.1.[1] During the forty years under survey there has been a steady decline in the percentage of the total of all farms ranging from 100 acres to 499 acres, and a steady and notable increase in those from 500 to 999 acres.[2]

Three questions present themselves. What are the causes of this movement toward larger farms? Has the larger farm come to stay? What effect, if any, has the increased size of farms on land tenure? Developments within the several counties of the state will be helpful in answering these questions.

North Dakota has fifty-three counties. Of these, forty-seven have maintained their boundaries unchanged during the decade to 1920, and two (Billings and Morton) have been divided and new counties formed. Sioux and Grant counties were organized from portions of Morton County, and Golden Valley and Slope Counties from Billings. So when comparison is made for the years 1910 and 1920 it is necessary to unite the 1920 figures for Golden Valley and Slope Counties to those of Billings, and similarly build up the figures for Morton County by the addition of figures for Sioux and Grant Counties.

Thus forty-nine counties may be compared. Comparison reveals that farms have increased in size in thirty-three counties, and have decreased in size in the remaining sixteen. In the United States Census for 1910 is the following

[1] *Fourteenth Census of the United States*, 1920 Bulletin, Agriculture: North Dakota, p. 3.

[2] United States Census figures on the size of farms in North Dakota are as follows:

	1880	*1890*	*1900*	*1910*	*1920*
100–499 acres	92.2	91.2	81.2	77.2	69.0
500–999 acres	2.7	5.0	11.3	17.0	23.7

From *Fourteenth Census of the United States*, Bulletin, Agriculture: North Dakota, p. 4.

comment upon the increase of the size of farms to that time:[1]

The increase may be accounted for by the fact that at the earlier dates there was a large proportion of farms which had been acquired from the Government and were still of the original size, usually 160 or 320 acres. These tracts have been united in many cases into larger farms as a result of the requirements of the wheat growers and live-stock farmers.

It is very probable that the growth of acreage in farms in the decade following the writing of the above statement was the result of similar circumstances. In the decade to 1920 the tractor and the large type of machinery made possible through its use, have no doubt played their part in accelerating the growth of farms. The tractor has offered an attractive method of partially solving the vexatious hired-help problem. But other things being equal, the tractor can be used most economically on the larger farms. The result is a continued and notable increase in the size of farms in thirty-three counties of the state.

But what of the other sixteen counties in which the average acreage per farm has actually decreased in the decade to 1920?[2] If the reader will consult a map of North Dakota he will see that these sixteen counties are clustered together and form, in a rough way, the eastern quarter of the state. This appears significant. These counties embrace the most fertile, oldest and best developed, as well as the most diversified area of the state. May this not well indicate that the increased average size of farms is only temporary and depends on the continuance of "one crop" farming? May it not indicate that 466.1 acres is too large an average for the

[1] *Thirteenth Census of the United States*, 1910, vol. vii, p. 273.

[2] The sixteen counties are Barnes, Benson, Cass, Dickey, Foster, Grand Forks, Griggs, La Moures, Nelson, Pembina, Ransom, Sargent, Steele, Traill, Walsh and Wells.

future in which it is to be hoped that the produce of the farms will become highly diversified?

There is apparently no connection between size of farms and tenancy. For just as strong a movement toward increased tenancy is seen in the counties where farms are decreasing in size as in the much more numerous counties where a notable increase in farm size is observed. Besides the average size of owners' farms increased considerably more than did the average size of tenants' farms. Owners' farms increased in average size from 373.1 acres in 1910 to 471.7 acres in 1920, while tenants' farms increased in average size from 409.1 acres to only 429.4 acres during the same period.[1]

LAND TENURE

When a new territory of farm land is opened for settlement, according to the methods of our Government, land is so easily acquired that tenancy is rare. Renting becomes more and more common as the communities become settled and land values enhance. The following table designed to show the development of land tenure in North Dakota through the past forty years forms an interesting basis for some observations concerning tenancy.[2]

Year	Total Number of Farms	Owners	Per Cent	Farms Operated by			
				Tenants	Per Cent	Managers Included with farms operated by owners	Per Cent
1880	3,790	3,712	97.9	78	2.1	....	..
1890	27,611	25,698	93.1	1,913	6.9	...	..
1900	45,332	40,972	90.4	3,865	8.5	495	1.1
1910	74,360	63,212	85.0	10,664	14.3	484	0.7
1920	77,690	56.917	73.3	19,918	25.6	855	1.1

[1] *Fourteenth Census of the United States*, 1920 Bulletin, Agriculture: North Dakota, p. 5.

[2] *Ibid.*, p. 4.

The number of farms operated by managers is so small, comparatively, as to warrant our neglecting it in discussing the growth of tenancy. Throughout the entire period a steady increase in the number of farms is noticeable. This, coupled with the observation made above that farms were increasing in size, leads to the conclusion that new lands are still being opened. The farms operated by owners grew rapidly and steadily until 1910, while the farms operated by tenants grew in even more rapid proportion (as indicated by the steadily rising percentage of all farms) and continued unabated to the present. Especially noteworthy is the fact that during the last decade the number of farms operated by owners has suffered a considerable decline in spite of the increase in the number of all farms. It is difficult to say just what is the full significance of this development. At all events its result is greatly to accelerate the movement toward tenant farming.

MORTGAGE INDEBTEDNESS AND CREDIT PRACTICES

We pass now to an investigation of the indebtedness of the land-owning North Dakota farmer. In 1890 North Dakota farms were mortgaged for $11,168,854, in 1910 for $47,841,587, in 1920 for $108,284,682.[1] Expressed in percentage of the total number of farms in the state, the farms encumbered with a mortgage comprise 48.7, 31.4, 50.9 and 75.9 per cent respectively.[2] More significant still are the ratios of mortgage debt to the value of the farms. In 1890 the per cent of value of the farm that was mortgaged was 14.8, in 1910, 22.4 and in 1920, 28.5 per cent.

[1] The United States Census does not give the mortgage indebtedness for 1900.

[2] The United States Census does not give the value of North Dakota farms for 1890. To get the percentage of farm value encumbered by mortgage it was necessary to resort to figures in the *Statistical Abstract of the United States*, 32nd number, 1909.

In North Dakota the average farm mortgage runs for a little short of five years, and the average interest rate is about eight per cent. This eight per cent, however, does not represent the actual price of a loan to a farmer, for he invariably pays for the expense of abstracting the titles, examining the property and recording the mortgage. Moreover, especially in the newer sections bonuses are sometimes exacted, and it is customary to deduct the year's interest in advance so that the final cost of a loan comes considerably higher.[1]

The funds borrowed by the North Dakota farmers on their farm mortgages come from various sources. Two life insurance companies, the Union Central of Cincinnati and the North Western Mutual of Milwaukee, loan heavily in the state. Local banks use farm mortgages in borrowing money from banks in large cities outside the state or in other cases turn the mortgages over to trust companies and collect a commission from the farmer for placing the mortgage. Every town and village has its money-lender who acts as agent for foreign investors in farm mortgages.

Short-time loans are of two kinds—bank loans and book credit advanced by retail stores. The bank loan is made on the farmer's note, generally unsecured though often secured by a chattel mortgage. The average length of these loans is eight and a half months; the average interest rate 10.75 per cent as reported by banks and 11.07 per cent as reported by farmers.

Store or book credit is perhaps the more important of the two. Where money is scarce and interest rates high, farmers frequently avail themselves of the merchant's credit in

[1] Meyer Jacobstein, "Farm Credit in a Northwestern State," *The American Economic Review*, vol. iii, September, 1913. Jacobstein's figures compare favorably with those of the United States Department of Agriculture. Department Bulletin no. 384 gives the results of a study made in 1914-15. Interest plus commission averages 8.7 per cent for the state.

preference to that of the banker. This is not because it is cheaper, but because it appears so, or is easier to obtain. Eighty-seven per cent of the farmers buy farm machinery on credit. Perhaps even a greater per cent buy other supplies on time. The farmer usually intends to pay at harvest time, but due to crop failures, etc., interfering, the average duration of such loans is slightly over twelve months. Frequently a note is taken by the merchant which may bear interest from date or sometimes only after the farmer has failed to pay at the expected time (harvest). These notes usually bear somewhat more than ten per cent. In the matter of discounts for cash, there is no uniform practice although seven per cent seems to be the most common. This would bring the cash price of a $160 binder to $150. Discounts on wagons and plows are usually from three to five dollars.[1]

The source of credit for independent and cooperative elevators deserves notice at this point because of the intimate connection between them and the farmers.[2] It appears that the main source of funds for these institutions are the terminal commission houses to which the country elevators consign their grain. It must be understood that the commission houses do this banking business unwillingly and are forced to it by competition. The rates of interest that they charge are usually based on a spread of one per cent from the terminal bank rate. Thus, if a Minneapolis commission house pays the bank from which it borrows six per cent, the usual practice is to charge the country elevator

[1] In the preparation of the preceding three and one-half paragraphs the author has drawn heavily on an article by Meyer Jacobstein, "Farm Credit in a Northwestern State," *American Economic Review*, vol. iii, September, 1913. While much of this material would be out of date today, it nevertheless describes conditions as they existed in the years in which the Nonpartisan revolution was taking shape.

[2] Sources of the information in this paragraph, *Report of the Federal Trade Commission on the Grain Trade*, vol. i, p. 242; vol. ii, pp. 184-196.

about seven per cent. This usually affords little or no profit to commission houses as they borrow and lend under conditions that frequently wipe out the possible profit. The commission house borrows for a stated length of time; the elevator only for the actual time it uses the funds. The commission house pays its discount in advance; the elevator pays the interest at the maturity of the loan. Moreover, interest at the borrowing rate is frequently allowed the elevator for balances with the commission house, so that a loss might arise from that source. On the whole the interest rate that the country elevator pays the commission house is substantially less than that paid the local bank when funds are obtained from it. In 1918 the most prevalent rates charged by commission houses were six and seven per cent. At the same time the interest rate of the local banks was said to be higher, in many cases ten per cent. The local banks do not prove equal to the need. The commission house is forced against its will to advance funds for the marketing of the grain crop. The following chapter treats this aspect of the North Dakota farmer's problem in detail.

CHAPTER II

Politico-economic Conditions in North Dakota

MARKETING OF GRAIN

In marketing his grain the North Dakota farmer really avails himself of only two methods to any considerable extent; firstly, outright sale to the local buyer; and secondly, direct shipment to the terminal markets. Of these two, the first is far the more important.[1]

The local buyer may be any one of a half-dozen different types. He may be (1) the agent of a commercial line house organization with an elevator in the town, (2) the agent of a mill line house with an elevator there, (3) an individual mill buyer, (4) an independent grain buyer, or (5) a cooperative or farmers' elevator manager. All of these have their individual elevators wherever they operate. Distinguished from these are the buyers without elevator or warehouse facilities, known as scoopers, track-buyers, interior brokers, etc., but they are of relatively little importance as market factors in North Dakota and can therefore be neglected.

Of the above mentioned local houses the commercial line house is by far the most important. It constitutes 54.17 per cent of all elevators combined. Next in importance is the cooperative or "farmers'" house (23.71 per cent), which is followed by the independent (14.67 per cent), the mill

[1] While direct shipping is subordinate to selling to local buyers, still North Dakota leads every other state in this method of marketing. Out of a total of 811 elevators, 75.83 per cent report direct shipping by farmers. Of this group 87.64 per cent report only occasional direct shipments.

line (5.42 per cent), and the individual mill houses (1.81 per cent) in their order of importance.[1]

The reasons for the dominance of the commercial line elevator in North Dakota spring largely from the comparatively rapid development of the grain industry in the state. Local accumulations of capital were very scarce among the pioneers and what capital there was they usually invested in some necessary equipment on or about the farm. Nothing of importance, then, was left with which to build, equip, and operate the elevators. Consequently the construction of elevators through the state and the purchasing of grain through them was necessarily carried on with Eastern capital. So it happened that large companies with central offices in one or the other of the terminal markets[2] built and operated large lines of elevators through the state. Their purpose was simply to merchandise in grain, buying from the farmer through their country elevator and shipping the grain to a terminal market to be sold at a profit. A few of these companies own and operate upwards of 150 country elevators each, the buying and selling operations of all country elevators being supervised by the central offices.

The reasons for the important development of the commercial line houses in North Dakota are at once the reasons for the comparative scarcity of independently owned elevators. Indeed it may safely be said that the lesser average capacity of the independently owned elevators is a result of the greater difficulties in securing capital under which their owners labor.[3]

The mill line and the individual mill houses are owned by milling interests mainly in Minneapolis. Their purpose is

[1] *Report of the Federal Trade Commission on the Grain Trade*, vol. i, p. 15.

[2] Minneapolis mainly.

[3] *Report of the Federal Trade Commission on the Grain Trade*, vol. i, p. 63.

to furnish the mills with their grinding requirements. They sometimes do a merchandising business also, but whenever they do, it is decidedly subordinated to their main function as an adjunct to the milling business. Consequently the mill elevator confines itself almost entirely to the purchase of wheat, and its average capacity is not high.[1]

Cooperative or "farmers'" elevators are, as indicated above, second in numerical importance in the state. Their relative importance is really still greater than their numerical percentage (23.71) indicates, because their average capacity is considerably larger than any other type. Cooperative elevators are of greater capacity probably because they expect to handle the greater share of the grain in the towns in which they operate and because their stockholder clientele is more stable and sure.

The important growth of cooperative elevators in the state is due to a feeling among farmers that they were not being paid fair prices for their grain by the line elevators. It was felt that there was a lack of competition among the buyers of grain. True, there were usually two or more elevators in a town, but it was felt that there was virtually no competition because of understandings and agreements between the various lines. Testimony before the Interstate Commerce Commission in November, 1906 proved that these suspicions were not without foundation. Mr. A. G. Hoskins testified that for about ten years preceding 1905 he had had charge of arrangements for dividing business at country stations, for sending out common price lists, for paying penalties on surplus grain purchased and for pooling grain. These activities of Hoskins were in behalf of not less than thirty-nine elevator companies with home offices in Minneapolis, and operating lines of country elevators throughout Minnesota, North Dakota and South Dakota, totaling about nine

[1] *Report of the Federal Commission, op. cit.*

hundred and fifty.[1] Surely here was machinery for exercising monopoly power in grain buying.

The cooperative elevators were established in many places with the hope of breaking the buying monopoly which apparently existed, and thus reducing the margin between the terminal market price and the price paid to farmers. Whether or not they have been successful in this is not certain. For, while many witnesses before the Interstate Commerce Commission in 1906 testified that the organization of a cooperative elevator resulted in a one to four cent rise in the price of grain at that point, the Federal Trade Commission in summing up conclusions regarding price margins states that "Some doubt may be expressed that on the whole the cooperatives . . . buy on much narrower margins, or in other words, pay the farmer appreciably more for his grain than do the other types," and "That in so far as the farmers do better by selling to the cooperative or farmers' elevators it is probably due to the returns derived by the customers in the form of dividends either on patronage or stock owned rather than to better prices paid the farmer at the time the grain is sold." [2] But on the whole there can be no doubt that the presence of the cooperative elevator stimulated the price of wheat because of the competition it engendered between itself and the old line houses, and if, as suggested above, the margins were about the same, it was a lower margin than would have existed in the absence of the cooperative company.[3]

[1] Sen. Doc. 278, 59th Cong., 2d Sess., pp. 930-964.

[2] *Report of the Federal Trade Commission on the Grain Trade*, vol. i, p. 194.

[3] The following letters taken by the Federal Trade Commission from the correspondence of the line elevator companies and reproduced in the *Report of the Federal Trade Commission on the Grain Trade*, vol. i, pp. 260, 276 and 280 substantiate this conclusion.

Some writers are inclined to lay great stress on the injustices to farmers of grain prices and grades because of the lack of local competition. Thus C. E. Russell in his book, *The Story of the Nonpartisan League,* uses his entire second chapter to show how the farmer of two decades ago in western North Dakota was caught in the meshes of a price fixing and grading combination of Minneapolis capitalists. This is perhaps an extreme case. At all events it is impossible to believe that it was typical of the state during the last

Atlantic Elev. Co., Crosby, N. D., Oct. 24, 1919
Minneapolis, Minn.
Dear Sir: The Farmers Elevator here is paying $2.56 for wheat—being 10c over card price, and $4.00 for flax—being 11c over card price. We have all been card price on flax and 5c over on wheat, and the Farmers Elevator is getting the biggest part of the grain at that . . . .
Yours very truly,
J. A. Kappadall.

H. J. Thorstenson, Agt., Nov. 1, 1916.
Northwood, N. D.
Dear Sir: Replying to yours of the 31st would say that I presume you cannot help but follow the prices being paid by the Farmers Elevator Co., but we hope that they will be agreeable to taking the stuff at list price.
Yours truly,
Andrew Grain Co.
BCC-Mc By

(From the files of the Victoria Elevator Company)
Sept. 5th, 1914.
Jacob Strobel,
Agt., Oriska, N. Dak.
Dear Sir: We saw a letter the Andrews Grain Co. received from their agent in which he says the Farmers are paying 3c over list for Barley, and they have written their man to meet competition and take their share of the stuff. Now you understand this matter, and it is a question of working together and keeping from cutting each others throat, but I think you are the oldest man there and have had a lot of experience and can keep them in line. We want to get some grain, and take it up to an even thing if necessary, but do not pay over other line buyers, but work with them.
Yours very truly,
RGc. MBL

decade when the Nonpartisan League was formed and the institutions under study operated. The Federal Trade Commission has collected a great bulk of evidence on this point by direct interviews and by combing the correspondence files of many of the old line companies operating in North Dakota. A review of this evidence leaves the very lasting impression that for the most part a very real and effective competition in the local purchase of grain existed or threatened to exist everywhere; that the large line companies were constantly confronted with the necessity of bringing competing companies to a buying understanding; and that while they were frequently successful in bringing about understandings among commercial line elevator interests, they found the cooperatives hard to deal with.[1] This competition

[1] The following letters reproduced in the *Report of the Federal Trade Commission on the Grain Trade*, vol. i, pp. 261, 268, 279, 281 are of interest.

(From the files of the Northwestern Elevator Company)

Grain Bulletin, Nov. 2 (?), 1917.
Chamb. of Com., City.

Gentlemen: Will you please take up with the Millers' Committee in relation to Casselton, N. D.? This mill is operated by Baldwin, and they are paying $2.10 for wheat regardless of the amount of inseparable matter it may contain, and drawing wheat 5 or 6 miles to the south of Everest and all around that country. . . . . .

Yours truly,
(unsigned) Gen. Supt.

Arthur, N. D. 8/26/19.

The St. Anthony has agreed to come to list, but we can't do anything with the Farmers Elev. Agent, but we are going to pay list after today and see how it works out.

Yours truly,
(signed) H. W. Buchanan

F. J. Pottner, Agt., Oct. 8, 1915.
Oriska, N. D.

Dear Sir: We have yours of the 6th stating that you and the Monarch agent are paying over list, and probably overgrading as well. I told you that under no circumstances would we care to have you overgrade, but you might meet competition on price.

which apparently was constantly harassing the elevators, was not only from those actually existing at a local station, but included elevators at other nearby stations where the trade would go if a difference in price of a cent or two was maintained.[1] It also included potential competition and,

Why is it that you and the Monarch agent are paying over list after you all apparently agreed not to do that?

Yours truly,

Andrews Grain Co.,

Bcc.Mc By

(From the files of the St. Anthony & Dakota Elevator Company)

Nov. 17, 1913.

Northwestern Elevator Company,
Minneapolis, Minn.
A. A. Magnuson

Gentlemen: We are enclosing you copy of letter from our Mr. Sheffield in regard to conditions at Hillsboro. Now, I believe you look at Hillsboro just as we do. It's anything to get that stuff away from the Farmers house, and we are trying to do that and not interfere with anyone else's business, and I think we have been able to make quite a hole in their business so far, without paying much attention to what your agent has done, but it would seem that in the future we should try and maintain the list price there and let the man that can get the stuff get it, I don't care whether it is you or ourselves. At any point where we have got Farmers' competition and where they are getting all the business, it's the live wire at the station who should get the business and not be hampered by the rest of us. I think you will agree with us on this.

Yours truly,

C. D. Junkin, Gen'l Supt.

[1] Evidence of this is seen in the following letters taken from the correspondence of line elevator companies and reproduced in the *Report of the Federal Trade Commission on the Grain Trade*, vol. i, pp. 249, 250.

(Andrews Grain Co. Receivers and shippers of grain)

General Office, Minneapolis, Minn.

To Andrews Grain Co., Oriska, N. D. Station, 11/1/15
Minneapolis, Minn.

Gentlemen: I received your letter dated 10/30 and noted contense. First plase we dident start with other people and pay Minneapolis prices then when we did get started we tried to get it on grade and next thing got together and bought on card prices and all the naboring towns paid more then Oriska. Now Monarch agt breaks agreement and Mr. O. Shea said

especially where there was a possibility of a cooperative or patronage dividend sharing elevator, the effect on the grain price margin was very real.[1]

While there apparently has been considerable competition in local buying throughout the last decade, it cannot be denied that the old line companies were doing their best to reduce this as much as possible. They were, as has been seen, not extremely successful in their efforts to bring about more uniformity of action on the part of the competitors. Still, they were constantly working toward some sort of mutual understanding and agreement with respect to

I could follow suit today the Farmers are haveing a meeting to compell the agent to buy 11 off on list from highest arive price. Now I am busy letting the farmers know that I will meet all comers if within reason almost half off the farmers are hauling to naboring towns that should haul here and it takes time to get them back. . . . . . .

Yours truly,

(signed) F. J. Pottner, agt.

The Northwestern Elevator Company

Minneapolis, Minnesota, Oct. 31, 1917.

National Elevator Co.
Monarch Elevator Co.

Gentlemen: Are we to understand you have come to list at Christine, N. D.? Christine is in competition with our Walcott station, and we would be glad to come to list immediately at Walcott if we can rely upon the fact that Christine will remain at list also.

Yours truly,

M. G. Magnuson, Gen. Supt.

(Taken from the files of the Empire Elevator Company)

August 31, 1914.

Mr. H. Thompson,
Oakes, N. D.

Dear Sir: We want you to use your influence to keep the market down at Ellendale. We do not want any fighting going on there, or the first thing we know, we will have to put the price up at Winship. . . . .

Yours truly,

JRM.M

[1] There are included in this description of price competition several different manifestations of the same phenomenon: namely, high prices, high weights, high grades, high grade services.

prices to be paid the farmers. The goal that they were striving toward was that all should buy according to "The Card."

Information concerning prices paid at terminal markets and which form the basis for local price quotations is received by country elevators in more than a half-dozen ways.[1] Most important of these in North Dakota are the price cards. These are usually post cards on the backs of which are printed the terminal market price quotations for the various kinds and grades of grain. Frequently future as well as cash prices are quoted, and, for full measure, some little trade gossip is added. These are mailed to the local elevators by the large commission houses.

By far the most influential of these cards is the one sent out by F. R. Durant of *The Grain Bulletin.*[2] This is known as the "Grain Bulletin Daily Price Card" or, as has already been suggested, throughout North Dakota it is more commonly known as "The Card". "The Card" is in many cases supplemented by *The Grain Bulletin's* wire service.

A significant difference between the ordinary price cards and the one released by *The Grain Bulletin* is that the former quote only terminal prices, leaving it to the local buyer to compute the price at which he could offer to buy grain at his office. The local buyer would then have to make allowances for shrinkage, freight, operating expenses and net profit before he could arrive at a price to be paid by him. The great variable—net profits—was left to his own judgment when he was determining the price margin. But Durant's Card goes further than to merely quote terminal prices. It at-

[1] *Report of the Federal Trade Commission on the Grain Trade*, vol. i, p. 181.

[2] 96 per cent of elevators in North Dakota report use of price cards. Of these 96 per cent, 96.84 per cent report the use of the Grain Bulletin Price Card. See *Report of the Federal Trade Commission on the Grain Trade*, p. 182.

tempts to quote prices which can actually be used for buying in the local market. In other words, " The Card " quotes prices which have already suffered reduction from terminal prices by the amount of freight from the local station, allowance for shrinkage, operating expenses, net profits, etc. The price margin between terminal and local markets is fixed. Here now is an attractive instrument for buying firms, weary of competition, to work with. Can they influence " The Cards " quotations so as to leave a handsome profit on the grain bought, and can they compel local competitors to adhere to " The Card " prices? A good deal of monopoly power might result if it were possible.

The Grain Bulletin's office from which "The Card" emanates is in Minneapolis. So are the main offices of most of the line elevator companies from which buying and selling operations of the various country branches are supervised. This is, of course, as it should be. The impression should not be formed that, because of the propinquity of the head offices of the great line elevators and the local price-quoting organ, there necessarily follows a price-fixing combination which determines upon a monopoly price. On the other hand, no one should be surprised if Mr. Durant and the heads of these commercial line elevators cooperated in an attempt to arrive at satisfactory price quotations. In fact, there is evidence that Durant held weekly meetings with the operators of certain important elevator companies " for consultation of matters of general interest." [1] Just what

[1] The following letter from the Cargill Elevator files is reproduced in the *Report of the Federal Trade Commission on the Grain Trade*, vol. i, p. 270.

Minneapolis, Minn.,
Sept. 17, 1915.

Cargill Elv. Co., D. D. McMillan
Imperial Elv. Co., P. L. Howe
Monarch Elv. Co., A. Stewart
National Elv. Co., L. D. Marshall

the "matters of general interest" involved is a matter of speculation. On the one hand the meetings may have been held for no other reason than to give Durant information necessary to the editing of an intelligent price card which would have been difficult to obtain except through these line elevator heads. On the other hand, there might have been a view to price fixing. At all events it is certain that "The Card" prices are employed as a basis of agreements among competitors, and in the correspondence between head offices and local line houses concerning price agreements the expression "buying to Card" or "to list" is continually in evidence and to get every one to buy to Card is the goal sought.[1] However, as has already been said, local competition was satisfactory enough as it affected the average North Dakota farmer.

THE TERMINAL MARKET SITUATION

We now shift our investigation to the terminal cities where the buying and selling forces operate which finally determine the price paid to farmers for their grain. About 88.93 per cent of North Dakota country elevator shipments go to terminal markets. Two are of importance, Minneapolis and Duluth, for between these two cities practically all of North Dakota's grain is divided. Since they are practically equi-distant from many of the northwestern shipping points, their respective growths as grain markets closely parallel each other. Their respective importance as measured by volume of grain received, appears below. Average

Northwestern Elv. Co., C. A. Magnuson
St. A & D Elv. Co., C. A. Brown

At a meeting held about a week ago, it was suggested that the companies named above meet each Friday afternoon at 3 o'clock in my office, for consultation of matters of general interest.

Please be represented this afternoon.

F. R. Durant

[1] See the correspondence in preceding foot-notes.

annual receipts for the five calendar years 1913-1917 were as follows: [1]

		Minneapolis	Duluth
Wheat	(Bu.)	120,151,000	56,884,000
Oats	"	30,446,000	5,624,000
Barley	"	33,171,000	11,424,000
Flaxseed	"	8,029,260	8,034,751
Rye	"	6,882,000	3,229,000

The Minneapolis market has always been practically coincident with the Minneapolis Chamber of Commerce.[2] The Chamber of Commerce originated in 1881 when various grain dealers organized for the purpose of facilitating their buying and selling of grain. On December 31, 1917, the classification of resident members in the grain trade of the Chamber were, according to the Federal Trade Commission, as follows: [3]

	Exclusively	*Primarily*	*Total*	*Secondary*
Cash Commissions	0	157	157	112
Terminal elevators	25	91	116	53
Other dealers[4]	10	3	13	14
Consumers[5]	59	3	62	7
Line elevators	26	43	69	68
Shippers[6]	8	4	12	58
Future Commissions[7]	31	4	35	283
	159	305	464	595
Out of town members; other exchanges 38, surrounding country 34			72	
Not in grain business			22	

[1] *Report of the Federal Trade Commission on the Grain Trade*, vol. ii, tables 2, 4, 5, 6, 52.

[2] "It has been publicly stated by officers of the Chamber that all the grain buyers of consequence within 150 miles of Minneapolis are members of the Chamber of Commerce." *Report of the Federal Trade Commission on the Grain Trade*, vol. ii, p. 152.

[3] *Ibid.*, vol. ii, p. 143.

[4] Feeders, primarily.

[5] Millers, maltsters, linseed crushers, etc.

[6] Operating without terminal facilities.

[7] Including one wire house.

This table shows clearly the predominance of the cash commission business. It is interesting to note that the tendency of the last dozen years has been strongly to foster selling on consignment.

The Manager of *The Grain Bulletin* at Minneapolis, which supplies the tributary areas with price information, reports that whereas "in 1907-1908, 75 per cent of the card quotations were sent to elevators controlled by line companies, today (1919) almost 75 per cent are sent to the operators of farmer's and independent elevators." It has been asserted by two well-known commission houses of Minneapolis that the growth of the commission business has been closely related to the farmer's cooperative elevator movement, and that the commission men have financed and otherwise assisted farmers' elevator companies, and built up a large consignment business at the expense of the line companies.[1]

Furthermore, a great deal of the grain coming in from line elevator branches in the country is sold on consignment. The line elevator companies, indeed, frequently being cosubsidiary companies along with commission houses, mills, terminal elevators, etc.

The reason for this great growth of the consignment business lies in the fact that seventy per cent of the wheat coming into the Minneapolis market is bought for local consumption. The big mills are prejudiced against terminal elevator mixed grain, far preferring to buy their grinding requirements on track by sample as the cars come in from the country. Hence the cash grain market of the Minneapolis exchange has had the commission house predominantly on the seller's side; and on the buyer's side the representatives of the milling, malting, and other consuming

[1] *Report of the Federal Trade Commission on the Grain Trade*, vol. ii, pp. 143, 144.

houses. The terminal elevator houses, at least as far as Minneapolis was concerned, could buy only the surplus not desired by the mills. These, together with the line elevator companies, trade on both sides of the market.[1]

The grievance of the North Dakota farmers with respect to the terminal markets were as follows: Firstly, they felt that injustice was being done them by questionable weights and grading. This they felt was particularly onerous in cases of direct shipments by farmers or shipments by cooperative or farmers' elevators. Secondly, they felt that the commission houses to which they consigned grain were not always as alive to the farmers' interests as they might have been. They believed that the commission houses frequently sold a shipment of grain by sample on the floor of the Chamber of Commerce to a fellow member with common interests, for far less than it was worth. Again the farmers felt that their grain passed through far too many hands on its way from their farm to the ultimate consumer. The farmers had plenty of grounds for their suspicions. The very intricate interlocking of the various interests on the Chamber floor was enough to excite suspicion and little investigation was needed to prove that in many cases too much was shaved off from the price that the consumer paid before the returns of a crop of grain came into the hands of the farmers.[2]

[1] *Report of the Federal Trade Commission on the Grain Trade*, vol. ii, pp. 144, 145.

[2] The memberships of the Pillsbury Flour Mills Company interests in the Minneapolis Chamber of Commerce and the Duluth Board of Trade afford a good example of the manner in which mills, elevators, and commission houses dealing on the grain exchanges were bound together by common ownership. A list of the memberships of this group follows:

To combat this combination on the home field cooperative

Pillsbury Flour Mills Co.
- J. W. Avery
- Edw. M. Kauth
- A. C. Loring
- A. F. Pillsbury
- Chas. S. Pillsbury
- Lester R. Stevens
- A. C. Loring *

Empire Elevator Co.
- J. R. McMillan
- E. N. Osborne
- Edward N. Osborne *

Atlantic Elevator Co.
- G. C. Bagley
- C. M. Case *

Union Terminal Elevator Co.
- W. F. Brittain
- R. W. Little

Kellogg Commission Co.
- Alvin F. Campbell
- Herbert A. Dew
- E. S. Ferguson *

Royal Elevator Co. and Geo. C. Bagley Elevator Co.
- R. C. Bagley
- C. M. Case
- R. C. Bagley *

Homestead Elevator Co.
- F. C. Riebe

Minneapolis & North Elevator Co.
- J. S. Pillsbury

Columbia Elevator Co.
- F. W. Commons
- H. W. Commons
- A. H. Thompson
- Victor Von Ende
- J. F. Whallon
- F. W. Commons *

* Members of Duluth Board of Trade, others members of Minneapolis Chamber of Commerce.

See the *Report of the Federal Trade Commission on the Grain Trade*, vol. ii, p. 151.

The farmers' attitude toward what they called the grain "combine" is well illustrated in the following letter taken by the Federal Trade Commission from the files of the Van Dusen-Harrington Company.

Fessenden, N. D., 11/6/17.

Mr. H. A. Fietus,
Minneapolis, Minn.

Dear Mr. Fietus: I want to ask you as a special favor not to use letter heads as per the enclosed in writing to any of my former elevator accounts, as it has the same effect on them as shaking a red cloth at a bull, as there is an awful strong sentiment among the average farmer elevator companies against commission houses who own a large line of old line elevators and letter heads like this certainly advertises us in good shape along this line.

Just to show you how a great many farmers organizations feel about

elevators were resorted to in large numbers, thus pretty effectively cutting down excessive buying margins in the country. But this was the smaller half of what would have been an effective remedy, for without adequate facilities to sell grain at the terminal markets even the cooperative elevator was useless. As has already been suggested, the method pursued by cooperative elevators and independent

doing business with what they call old line firms, the farmers organized at Armaurdale, N. D. I did not waste any time going to see them at all as I was told just what they were, but they made arrangements early with Kellogg Commission Co., and threw them over when they learned they owned the Atlantic Elev. Co., and made arrangements with the Brown Grain Co. only to learn later on that they were the St. Anthony & Dakota and finally landed with McCarthy Bros., a strictly commission house.

This crowd at Wimbleton are somewhat Equity inclined and the manager asked me today if Van Dusen-Harrington owned all these line of Elevators. I put him off by telling him you were joint traffic manager for all the above companies but I could see he did not seem satisfied and I know such letter heads as this should not be used in correspondence with our local shippers and I hope your stenographer will be instructed thoroughly so that they will not use it especially when writing to Farmers Elev. Co.

Yours truly,

(signed) E. O. Dilling

See the *Report of the Federal Trade Commission on the Grain Trade*, vol. ii, p. 264.

Andrews Grain Co.,
Northwood, N. D. Station, Jan. 16, 1913.

Andrews Grain Co.,
Minneapolis, Minn.

Dear Sirs: I have tried for a week to get some wheat at one cent over the price the rest is paying but can not tutch it at that I have talked to the farmers and asked them why they would not hall some here and they say they would sooner the Mill or the Farmers elevator would get it as they was run to protect the farmer.

Yours truly,

(signed) O. M. Lee

See the *Report of the Federal Trade Commission on the Grain Trade*, vol. ii, p. 264.

shippers was to consign their grain to a Chamber of Commerce commission firm, which sold the grain on the floor of the Chamber to whom they could or would.

These commission houses occupied a very powerful seat between farmer and consumer. The commission houses furnished a very important part of the funds needed by the independent and cooperative elevators during the crop-moving season.[1] Furthermore, it was difficult indeed to sell on the Chamber of Commerce floor without their offices, and to look for a market of any extent outside the Chamber was useless. There is considerable evidence to show that these commission houses frequently abused their power, and resorted to unfair methods of trade. As a result farmers often suffered severe losses.[2]

EARLY ATTEMPTS AT EMANCIPATION

In order to emancipate themselves from what they conceived to be a combination of interests on the floor of the Chamber of Commerce to strip them of all profits, the farmers of the Northwest attempted one or two interesting experiments. In 1903 about a dozen farmers of Clay County,

[1] *Report of the Federal Trade Commission on the Grain Trade*, vol. ii, pp. 235, 236.

[2] *Supra*, p. 50 note.

On the other hand there is evidence that commission houses gave good service. Thus, in a letter to the author, the Farmers Grain Co. of Devil's Lake writes as follows: "Our credit has been good with commission men with whom we have dealt, and we could not ask for better treatment than we have always received. The fact is our business is sought and competition for it insures us the best kind of treatment." These two opposing views of the commission houses may perhaps be reconciled by remembering that the interests of independent commission houses and commission houses that are subsidiaries of some large combination do not necessarily lie in the same direction. The treatment which a cooperative shipper would receive at the hands of a commission firm might well depend on whether the commission firm was related to a line elevator company with a country elevator in the same town.

Minn. (on the North Dakota line), banded themselves together for the purpose of improving the conditions under which they had to market their grain. They rightly saw that local action was useless unless they were sure of being able to dispose of their grain at a fair price and without paying too heavy commissions at the terminals. So they themselves bought a membership in the Minneapolis Chamber of Commerce which would entitle one of their own members or their chosen representative to go on the floor of the exchange and sell grain upon equal terms with the so-called "interests".[1] But this group of Clay County farmers was doomed to a rude awakening. Scarcely had they opened offices in Minneapolis and begun advertising for consignments of grain when they found that the fact that they owned a membership really meant but little because it could be annulled if the directors desired to do so. In other words, not only was it necessary to comply with the general rules of the Chamber, but an aspirant for a seat had to pass censorship by the board of directors.[2]

It is by no means clear upon what basis the Chamber denied the Minnesota Farmers Exchange full privileges of membership. Conflicting statements by the officials of the Chamber and of the Farmers Exchange somewhat befog the facts. The Chamber declared the farmers' organization was refused membership because upon investigation it proved to be insolvent.[3] The Minnesota Farmers Exchange asserted that the Chamber was satisfied with their representative and with their financial condition, but denied them corporate membership without ever intimating what was

[1] Russell, Charles Edward, *The Story of the Nonpartisan League* (New York, 1920), p. 114.

[2] Sen. Doc. 278, 59th Cong., 2nd Sess., pp. 293, 294, 1002.

[3] *Ibid.*, p. 1001.

the cause of their refusal.[1] A study of the testimony of the various witnesses called before the Interstate Commerce Commission when they were investigating the grain trade at Minneapolis in 1906 leaves the reader with the definite impression that in all probability the Chamber of Commerce was hostile to the idea of bringing into the membership of the Chamber any cooperative society of farmers which might lessen their monopolistic hold on grain marketing at the terminals.[2] The Minnesota Farmers Exchange went to pieces after a series of abortive attempts to gain membership in the Chamber of Commerce and after having sustained some heavy losses through irregularities of one of the grain houses connected with the Chamber of Commerce.[3]

Another attempt at more direct marketing was begun in 1907 when the Equity Society was organized as a grain-selling association. At first it undertook to sell the grain

[1] Sen. Doc. 278, 59th Cong., 2nd Sess., p. 993. The letter conveying the Board's decision to the Farmers Exchange was as follows:

July 18, 1905

Mr. L. K. Meyers,
Secretary Minnesota Farmers' Exchange, Corn Exchange, City.
Dear Sir: Your application for corporate membership for the Minnesota Farmers' Exchange was considered by the board of directors of the Chamber of Commerce of Minneapolis at a meeting yesterday, July 17, 1905, and the application was not granted.

Yours truly,
G. D. Roberts, Secretary.

[2] At the present time The Farmers Grain Co. of Devil's Lake reports that by virtue of memberships held in the name of its president, this co-operative organization pays to commission houses only half the regular commission. They report that they never have had reason to complain about the services of either the Chamber of Commerce or commission houses.

[3] Sen. Doc. 278, 59th Cong., 2nd Sess., p. 998.

Russell in his book *The Story of the Nonpartisan League* gives an excerpt from the Investigation of Exchanges; House of Representatives of Minnesota testimony, pp. 246, 247, that gives more evidence on this point.

consigned to it at Minneapolis through a regular grain dealer. In 1911 the form of the organization was changed to that of a corporation. This corporation, the Equity Co-operative Exchange, became exceedingly antagonistic to the Minneapolis Chamber of Commerce and in 1912 was practically barred from selling grain on the Chamber of Commerce floor. In 1914 the Equity moved to St. Paul and endeavored to wage the fight against the Chamber of Commerce with renewed vigor.[1] But its success has been limited. While it is still an active going concern there is little reason to believe that it will ever be sufficiently strong to wield an important influence over marketing conditions in North Dakota.

Beginning with 1907 a number of state laws were enacted and constitutional amendments ratified which were designed to remedy some of the more flagrant abuses of the terminal markets. In that year a law was passed providing that the governor of North Dakota should, upon request of the governor of Wisconsin, recommend one or more persons for appointment upon the Grain and Warehouse Commission of the City of Superior.[2] In 1909 another law was passed providing that the governor of North Dakota appoint expert representatives to sit with the Minnesota Board of Grain Appeals "and act as representatives of the grain shippers of North Dakota and look after their interests in all matters relating to inspection, weighing, grading and docking of grain shipped from North Dakota."[3] In 1912 a constitutional amendment was ratified which gave the legislative assembly authority and power "to provide by

[1] Boyle, James E., "The Agrarian Movement in the Northwest," *The American Economic Review*, vol. viii, no. 3, Sept., 1918.

[2] *The Compiled Laws of the State of North Dakota* (1913), Political Code, chap. 38, art. 79.

[3] *Ibid.*, Political Code, chap. 38, art. 73.

law for the erection, purchasing or leasing and operation of one or more terminal grain elevators in the state of Minnesota or Wisconsin or both. . . ."[1] In 1913 a law was passed providing that the State Board of Control investigate thoroughly the matter of location, cost of building and equipping, methods of operation and other facts, a knowledge of which would be helpful in successfully establishing and operating state terminal elevators in either Minnesota or Wisconsin or both states. Such information as the Board of Control could gather was to be imparted by it to the 1915 legislative assembly. It was further provided that beginning with 1914 and continuing through 1916 a special tax levy of one-eighth of one mill be placed on each dollar of the assessed valuation of all taxable property in the state for the purpose of creating a fund to be known as the "State Terminal Elevator Fund" which was to be used for the "erection, purchase, leasing, equipment, maintenance and operation of a terminal elevator system or systems" in the states mentioned above.[2] In 1913 another constitutional amendment was approved by the legislative assembly, and was ratified by the electors at the general election of 1914. This amendment authorized and empowered the legislative assembly "to provide by law for the erection, purchase or leasing and operation of one or more terminal grain elevators in the State of North Dakota."[3]

A review of the laws and constitutional amendments just described indicates that the state had by 1915 committed itself definitely to state-owned terminal facilities. The popularity of the scheme is shown by the popular vote on the two constitutional amendments. The one of 1912 had cast in its favor 56,488 and against it 18,864 votes, and the

[1] *The Compiled Laws of the State of North Dakota* (1913), p. cxii.

[2] *Ibid.*, Political Code, chap. 33.

[3] *Ibid.*, p. cxxvii.

amendment of 1914 was favored by 51,507 votes as against 18,483 opposed.[1]

One would naturally have expected the legislative session of 1915 actively to begin a program of state building. However, two occurrences blocked the way. The first was the election of the conservative L. B. Hanna to the governorship in the fall of 1914, the other was the report of the committee of the Board of Control created by the law of 1913. The committee reported that to their mind state-ownership of terminal elevators was unwise and that the matter should be left entirely to cooperative effort. A bitter fight ensued but the result was that the legislature finally adopted the report. Thus the scheme of state-ownership of terminal elevators had for the time being suffered defeat. The farmers were highly incensed. They felt that they had again been betrayed into the hands of the "interests" by the old parties. A crisis was imminent.

THE NONPARTISAN LEAGUE

Arthur C. Townley came to Bismarck early in 1915 to observe the farmers and the legislature.[2] He saw that the farmers were in a state of mind, with respect to the old parties which were defeating their cherished plans for better marketing conditions, that would make it very simple for a leader with a definite progressive program to enlist their votes and aid. Townley had been doing organization work among farmers for the socialist party the year before. He knew of the dissatisfaction toward old line parties and the

[1] Bruce, Andrew A., *Non-Partisan League*, New York, 1921; Langer, William, *The Nonpartisan League*, Mandan, 1920.

[2] In the preparation of this section the writer has drawn heavily upon the two books, *The Nonpartisan League* by H. C. Gaston, and *The Story of the Nonpartisan League* by C. E. Russell. These two men, and particularly Gaston, were in an excellent position to write on the beginnings of the League.

control that the eastern interests had held. He knew that with the recent strife in Bismarck between a conservative legislature and the Equity Society and its farm following, the time was ripe for a political revolution. He had furthermore observed the methods of the " interests ", in controlling affairs of the state. He had observed that whoever wished to control the affairs of the state saw to it that a man who would do their bidding was nominated at the primaries. To what particular political party he happened to belong was not of moment so long as he was pledged to follow their instructions. The importance of the control of the primary election therefore impressed itself deeply into Townley's mind and he resolved to so organize the farmers that they could do the dictating at the primaries, whether Republican, Democratic, or both. Hence the organization of the Farmers Nonpartisan League,[1] an organization designed to cement the farmers of the state together for united action in nominating at the primaries and electing at the polls men of their own choosing and men who would carry out their programs.

The method of organization was simple, scientific and successful. So-called organizers carefully trained in the art of salesmanship went forth in ever increasing numbers to sell the idea to the farmers and to get their support for the new movement.

The farmers became members of the League upon payment of the dues and by signing a pledge. The dues were modest at first—$2.50 a year. Shortly they were changed to six, and again to nine dollars a year. After that the dues were made to cover two years and sixteen dollars was the amount. The pledge was to " use their best efforts to secure the nomination and election of men for office within

[1] Later changed to National Nonpartisan League.

the state whom the investigations of this League show by conviction, record and conduct do approve and will support legislation necessary for the purposes above expressed." The "investigations" it was explicitly agreed upon were to be carried on by and under the supervision of an executive committee of five men. The "purposes above expressed" related to the savings of millions of dollars each year to the farmer and were to be effected through the carrying out of the league program.

The league program was concise and to the point. It consisted of five planks, as follows: [1]

1. State owned and operated elevators, flour mills, and packing plants;
2. State hail insurance;
3. Exemption of farm improvements from taxation;
4. Fair grain grades, based upon milling and baking values;
5. Rural credits at cost.

Each was designed to remedy what was conceived by the farmers as an abuse, and each was to lower the cost of producing and marketing grain.

The League grew with leaps and bounds. The first members were pledged in February, 1915. Before midsummer there were 10,000 members, and before winter set in there were 26,000 names enrolled.

The next general election at which the new League could test its strength was to come in November, 1916 with the primaries coming in June. As has been mentioned above, the League knew the importance of the primaries, for whomsoever they might choose then would have control of the state. A state convention was called to meet at Fargo to

[1] *The North Dakota Industrial Program*, The Industrial Commission of North Dakota, June 1, 1920.

nominate a state ticket. It consisted of one member from each legislative district. Whether or not these members had much to do with the nomination is not certain. It is fairly certain, however, that the executive committee of the Nonpartisan League formed a very effective steering committee and perhaps dictated the ticket. This state "ticket" was recommended to the Republicans as being the choice of the farmers and adopted by them. The result of the November elections was that every man indorsed by the Nonpartisan League save one, Casey for treasurer, was elected. The three candidates for the supreme court indorsed by the League were swept into office by impressive pluralities. The League elected eighty-seven representatives out of a possible hundred and thirteen. This overwhelming victory gave them a decided majority in the house. But the League elected only eighteen state senators and twenty-five were required for a majority in the senate.

A matter of first importance to this legislature was the amending of the state constitution so as to permit the farmers' program to be enacted into law. For as the constitution stood, about the only part of the program that could be carried out was that which pertained to the state-owned terminal elevator. For the rest, further constitutional authority was needed.

To bring about the necessary constitutional changes with despatch it was necessary for the legislature to pass a bill calling for a constitutional convention. Such a bill was introduced in 1917 in the house, but the bloc opposed to the league program prevented its passage in the senate. The consequence was that for the most part the League's program had to await the amendment of the constitution.

This could not be done during the 1917 session and consequently the laws enacted by this first farmers' legislature while remedying many minor abuses did not enact laws which put the main features of the league program into operation. These were not made possible until the legislative session of 1919 unhampered by constitutional restriction enacted laws creating and providing for the institutions and reforms advocated in their platform.[1] Among others, the law providing for the Bank of North Dakota was enacted at this session. It is with the operations of this institution that we will now concern ourselves.

[1] For a good short summary of both the 1917 and 1919 legislative sessions, see Bruce, *Non-Partisan League*, p. 88 and following.

CHAPTER III

Nonpartisan Legislation and the Bank Act

NONPARTISAN PROGRAM CRYSTALLIZED IN LAW

Thus far an attempt has been made to describe the soil from which the Nonpartisan revolution sprang, and briefly to recite the main features of the new state system championed by the League. This chapter aims to present the salient features of the laws creating the Bank and providing for its organization and operation.

The Nonpartisan industrial program received a hearty endorsement from Governor Frazier when he delivered his message at the opening of the 1919 legislative assembly. The Governor made specific mention of the desirability of legislation that would create a state bank, a state mill and elevator, compulsory state hail insurance, state lignite coal mines, a state home-building program, and an industrial commission to manage and operate the various state utilities.[1] The message fell, for the most part, on friendly ears. Both House and Senate busily prepared to enact the necessary legislation that would make the Nonpartisan industrial program a reality. The result was the enactment of laws;

1. Establishing the Bank of North Dakota;[2]
2. Providing for the issue of bonds, bank series;[3]

[1] *Journal of the House of the Sixteenth Session of the Legislative Assembly*, pp. 13-21.

[2] *Session Laws of 1919*, chap. 147.

[3] *Ibid.*, chap. 148.

3. Authorizing an experimental creamery;[1]
4. Establishing a Home Builders' Association;[2]
5. Creating an Industrial Commission;[3]
6. Creating a Mill and Elevator Association;[4]
7. Providing for an issue of bonds, mill and elevator series;[5]
8. Providing for an issue of bonds, real estate series;[6]
9. Amending the Hail Insurance Law so as to provide compulsory state hail insurance;[7]
10. Amending the law on exemption of property from taxation so as to exempt all structures and improvements on agricultural lands, and exemption from taxation of his tools and implements to the amount of one thousand dollars.[8]

The laws enumerated were the product of a revolutionary legislature. Such laws are extremely apt to be the expression of pent-up desires, thwarted plans, and idealistic dreams. The men responsible for their drafting and passage are likely to be in the mood that possessed Representative Caddell on the day that Governor Frazier signed the bills that established the state industrial program. When Governor Frazier had finished signing the bills, Lieutenant Governor Wood called on a number of senators and representatives to make a few remarks. Among others he called on Representative Caddell. Thereupon Mr. Caddell delivered himself of the following:

[1] *Session Laws of 1919*, chap. 149.
[2] *Ibid.*, chap. 150.
[3] *Ibid.*, chap. 151.
[4] *Ibid.*, chap. 152.
[5] *Ibid.*, chap. 153.
[6] *Ibid.*, chap. 154.
[7] *Ibid.*, chap. 160.
[8] *Ibid.*, chap. 223.

Mr. President, Governor, state officials, members of the joint session and citizens. Were I a painter I believe I could derive inspiration from what has been done here today to paint a great picture. Were I an orator I know of no greater subject were it left to me to choose. Being neither, however, I am going to quote a verse of scripture. This may not be exactly consistent, not being a minister of the gospel, but I think this verse of scripture, and I want to say that I have not got it exactly correct, expresses the way a great number of the people of North Dakota feel. I do not know the number of the verse, I do not know the number of the chapter, but it goes something like this: "This is the day that we long have sought, and mourned because we found it not."

Such legislators bring to their task the courage and zeal of crusaders. They know what conditions and institutions their program of reform calls for, but the means of attaining these ends are not so carefully considered. There is usually no close precedent from which to draw experience, so, while the end is well known, the means can merely be guessed at. Consequently the chief concern of the lawmakers is that no legislative restriction or technical matter shall block the way for important reforms and innovations. What is wanted, as far as legislation is concerned, are laws granting power to the new government, and not restricting it. Hence such legislation deals with generalities and leaves important matters of detail and policy to the judgment of those who must execute the laws. The laws providing for the state industrial program are eminently of this type. For the most part they deal with very general considerations only. Most of the policy, to say nothing of detail, is left to the judgment of the Industrial Commission. It is not surprising, therefore, to find legal provision made for an exceedingly autocratic control of the State Bank. Since so much is left to "sound judgment" when the occasion arises, the exercise of it must be the privilege of a small and compact group. Such a group is the Industrial Commission of North Dakota.

THE INDUSTRIAL COMMISSION OF NORTH DAKOTA

The Industrial Commission consists of three members, the governor, the attorney general and the commissioner of agriculture and labor. The governor is chairman, and the attorney general is attorney for the Commission. Two members constitute a quorum for the transaction of business, but the approval and signature of the governor is required before any important decision becomes effective. In other words, he can veto anything that the other two members of the Commission undertake to do. The governor is supreme in the Industrial Commission. The powers vested in it are virtually vested in the governor. It would, perhaps, be nearer the truth to say that the state industries are under the control of one man than to say that they are under the control of three.

The duties of the Industrial Commission are "to manage, operate, control and govern all utilities, industries, enterprises, business projects, now or hereafter established, owned, undertaken, administered or operated by the state . . . except those carried on in penal, charitable or educational institutions." [1] Here was heavy responsibility indeed, but powers are granted commensurate with the task. Specifically the grants of power are as follows:

1. To determine the location of the state industries and business enterprises;
2. To buy, lease, or acquire by exercise of the right of eminent domain any and every kind of property necessary for the state industries;

[1] *Session Laws of 1919*, chap. 151, sec. 5. The remainder of this paragraph is based on the same section.

3. To appoint managers, subordinate officers and employees for the several industries, who remain subject to the supervision, limitation and control of the Industrial Commission;
4. To remove and discharge any of the managers or employees of the industries;
5. To "fix the buying price of things bought and the selling price of things sold" incidental to these industries and business ventures: (this, of course, included the power to fix rates and charges for services rendered by the state utilities);
6. To "make rules, regulations, orders and by-laws for the management and operation, and for the transaction of business", of such industries and businesses;
7. To finance such utilities by the sale of state bonds as provided by law;
8. To conduct investigations bearing either directly or indirectly on the conduct of the state industries;
9. To make rules and regulations for its own procedure; and,
10. For good measure and to make certain that no limit under the sky be placed upon the powers of this Industrial Commission the law empowers it "to do any and all things necessary or expedient in conducting the business of such utilities, industries, enterprises, and business projects, and in accomplishing the purposes of the Act."

The legal checks on this tremendous grant of power are few and of little significance. The manner in which it is exercised is left in the main to the "sound judgment" of the Commission itself. The main check over its affairs consists in the necessity of the preparation of an annual report which must be filed with the Secretary of State. The law requires a rather elaborate report of the expenditures of the

Commission and detailed financial statements of the various industries under its control. Thus considerable publicity of its affairs is obtained, and some slight restraint over the abuse of power is secured.

THE ADMINISTRATION OF THE BANK

The administration of the Bank focuses in the Industrial Commission. To it the Bank Act delegates the responsibility of locating, operating, managing and controlling the Bank of North Dakota.[1] This being a large order, the legislature saw the necessity of granting the Industrial Commission abundant power and a comparatively free hand in affairs pertaining to the Bank. To facilitate the Commission's work in locating and maintaining a business site for the Bank, the law gives power to buy, lease, or condemn property and to construct or repair buildings for the purpose of housing the Bank. The only legal limitation to this power is that the main place of business shall be in North Dakota and that not more than $200,000 be spent in acquiring such a home for the Bank.[2]

The Bank Act supplies the Industrial Commission with an abundance of power to be exercised in operating, managing and controlling the Bank. To begin with, it is empowered to obtain such assistance as it deems necessary for the proper establishment and organization of the Bank. It is required that a manager be appointed to act as the Commission's general agent in affairs pertaining to the Bank. But with respect to subordinate officers and employees, the Industrial Commission is to use its good judgment in determining the number employed and salaries paid. The only restriction is that the total wage bill together with the other expenditures incident to the maintenance and opera-

[1] *Session Laws of 1919*, chap. 147, sec. 21.

[2] *Ibid.*, sec. 3.

tion of the Bank should " remain within the appropriation and earnings lawfully available in each year for the purpose." [1] Moreover the Industrial Commission may remove and discharge any appointee or employee connected with the Bank.[2] In short, it has legal authority to hire and fire the officers and employees of the Bank from director general to janitor.

Sprinkled here and there throughout the remaining sections of the Act is the authority for the Commission's assumption of many powers; and much is left to its " sound judgment ". Chief among these powers are the following:

1. To designate banks or agencies to receive deposits for the Bank; [3]
2. To determine the terms upon which the Banks, acting as a reserve bank, will rediscount paper, collect checks, etc.; [4]
3. To fix (within wide legal limits) rates of interest allowed and received, and charges made for services rendered; [5]
4. To determine the terms and conditions under which the Bank will deposit funds in local banks; [6]
5. To make terms and rules under which funds will be loaned to the various political subdivisions of the state, and to State and National Banks; [7]
6. To prescribe the form of application for a mortgage

[1] *Session Laws of 1919*, chap. 147, sec. 4.

[2] *Ibid.*, sec. 5.

[3] *Ibid.*, sec. 9.

[4] *Ibid.*, sec. 11.

[5] *Ibid.*, sec. 12.

[6] *Ibid.*, sec. 14.

[7] *Ibid.*, sec. 15.

loan on real estate, and to provide for appraisal of the proposed security;[1]

7. In case of crop failure to extend for one year the payments on mortgages;[2]
8. To order mortgages assigned to the state treasurer for use as security for real estate bonds issued by him.[3]

The Industrial Commission is, indeed, well equipped with legal authority to control the establishment and operation of the Bank of North Dakota.

CAPITAL

The Bank's capital was provided for in a separate act.[4] The state treasurer and governor were directed to issue state bonds to the sum of $2,000,000 and deliver them into the hands of the Industrial Commission. The Industrial Commission was directed to sell these bonds for cash in a manner and at terms that it might deem advantageous to the state. The act specifically declares that these bonds may be purchased with perfect propriety by the Bank itself with any funds in the Bank. The money derived from the sale of the bonds was to constitute the Bank's capital, and the Industrial Commission was directed to use it as such.

The bonds here described are the so-called Bank Series bonds. They were to be issued in denominations of from five to ten thousand dollars and were to mature in from ten to thirty years. Not more than six per cent interest, payable semi-annually, was to be paid. "The terms of the bonds as to values of denominations, periods of maturity and rates of interest" were to be fixed by the governor "in his sound judgment, within the limits above stated."[5]

[1] *Session Laws of 1919*, chap. 147, sec. 16.

[2] *Ibid.*, sec. 17.

[3] *Ibid.*, sec. 20.

[4] *Ibid.*, chap. 148.

[5] *Ibid.*, sec. 2.

The security of these bonds was the pledged faith and credit of the state. The funds with which the treasurer could meet the payment of interest and principal were to be provided in two ways. First, if the earnings of the Bank were sufficient to warrant a transfer of a part of them into the "Bank Bond Payment Fund," the Industrial Commission had authority to do so. Secondly, if the earnings of the Bank were not sufficient to meet the requirements of interest and principal payments, the State Board of Equalization was directed to levy an annual tax sufficient in amount to cover the deficit in the sum needed to pay interest. In addition, the State Board of Equalization was directed to levy a state tax, annually, during the last five years before the maturity of any of the bonds, which together with money paid by the Industrial Commission for the purpose would be sufficient to retire one-fifth part of the bonds. In case the Bank Bond Payment Fund was temporarily embarrassed by reason of the failure of the above mentioned sources to furnish funds, then the state treasurer is called upon to "supply the deficiency out of any other available moneys of the state in his custody." These funds were to be returned as soon as possible to the sources whence taken.

GENERAL BANKING POWERS GRANTED BY THE BANK ACT

The 1919 legislature granted general banking powers with characteristic prodigality. With but minor exceptions, "The business of the Bank . . . may include anything that any bank may lawfully do."[1] Specific mention is made of the power to receive deposits, to exercise the usual powers of a central reserve bank, to re-deposit funds and to make mortgage and commercial loans. These may now be taken up in greater detail.

[1] *Session Laws of 1919*, chap. 147, sec. 2.

DEPOSITS

As a matter of convenience we may divide the deposits that the Bank is authorized to receive, into two classes, public and private. By public deposits is meant all state, county, township and school-district funds as well as the funds of all penal and public educational and industrial institutions, which the law required to be deposited in the Bank of North Dakota. By private deposits is meant deposits of funds of private individuals, corporations or associations.

One of the most revolutionary phases of the Bank Act was the section which compelled all treasurers having public funds in their custody to deposit them in the Bank, on pain of fine and imprisonment.[1] This sweeping provision included public sinking funds as well as funds for current needs. Hence both time and demand deposits were to be received from public sources. These deposits when added together were always sure to be a substantial basis upon which the Bank could rely. If private depositors remained hostile, timid, or indifferent, the Bank would not be embarrassed by lack of working funds. Moreover these funds were attracted to the Bank without expense. No interest need be paid to satisfy the law, although the Industrial Commission might allow interest from one to six per cent if it seemed wise. No competition exacted favorable terms, for the public treasurers were without choice in the matter.

Concerning private deposits no such arbitrary rulings could be made. Private deposits must be attracted through making the conditions of deposit more attractive than could be found elsewhere. Accordingly all deposits are guaranteed by the state and are exempted from state, county and municipal taxes.[2] Provision is made so that the Industrial

[1] *Session Laws of 1919*, chap. 147, sec. 7.

[2] *Ibid.*, sec. 10. It should be said that all deposits both public and private enjoy the state's guarantee and are exempt from state, county and municipal taxation.

Commission may pay a liberal rate of interest.[1] A special inducement is offered to state banks. Funds which they deposit in the Bank of North Dakota are to be considered "available funds" or lawful reserve. To such banks as made it their legal depositary the Bank of North Dakota might "perform the functions and render the services of a clearing house, including all facilities for providing domestic and foreign exchange," and rediscount paper on terms made by the Industrial Commission.[2]

RESERVE

Summing up what has thus been given in detail, it may be said that the Bank Act provided for public and permitted private deposits many of which were demand obligations of unusual importance. Where so much depended on prompt payment of deposits a strict reserve requirement might have been expected. But the Bank Act will be searched in vain for even a hint at a cash reserve. The omission from the Act of some sort of a reserve requirement is another one of the amazing circumstances which left the Bank at the mercy of the Industrial Commission.

LOANS

Next, consider what may lawfully be done with these widely differing types of deposits. The reader should bear in mind that there is nothing in the law requiring that a distinction be made with respect to either the source or kind of deposit. Demand or time, public or private, state bank reserve or individual saving deposits are all as one in the law.

Perhaps there is no briefer way to present the legal provisions concerning bank loans than to quote from the Act itself:

[1] *Session Laws of 1919*, chap. 147, sec. 12.

[2] *Ibid.*, sec. 11.

The Bank of North Dakota may transfer funds to other departments, institutions, utilities, industries, enterprises or business projects of the State, which shall be returned with interest to the Bank. It may make loans to counties, cities or political subdivisions of the State, or to State or national banks, on such terms, and under such rules and regulations, as the Industrial Commission may determine; but it shall not make loans or give its credit to any individual, association or private corporation, except that it may make loans to any individual, association or private corporation, secured by duly recorded first mortgages on real estate in the State of North Dakota in amounts not to exceed one-half the value of the security, or secured by warehouse receipts issued by the Industrial Commission or by any licensed warehouse within the State, in amounts not to exceed ninety per cent of the value of the commodities evidenced thereby. It shall not, however, loan on real estate security more than thirty per cent of its capital, nor in addition thereto, more than twenty per cent of its deposits. Additional funds, that may be required for such real estate loans, shall be procured from the sale of State bonds as may be provided by law.[1]

The section suggests possibilities. There is nothing in the law to prevent the bank officials from loaning a state bank's legal reserve on a farm mortgage; or the current funds of a state educational institution to a state industry for permanent investment. The confusion of deposits and the promiscuous loaning of them, while perfectly lawful, brought misery a-plenty to the Bank. In another chapter it will be shown how the misapplication of deposits so nearly wrecked the Bank.

Much space is given to an elaboration of the way in which the real estate mortgage loans are to be made, and the manner in which other funds should be secured for additional loans. But despite the fact that the law goes into consider-

[1] *Session Laws of 1919*, chap. 147, sec. 15.

able detail at this point, much of importance is left for the Industrial Commission to determine. After reading the sections of the Bank Act that deal with the farm mortgage loans, the impression remains that the legislators were not sure of their ground and therefore decided to leave important decisions to the Industrial Commission, the members of which could decide upon policy as necessity arose.

REDISCOUNTS AND REDEPOSITS

Two other aspects of the disposition of deposits deserve mention here. One has to do with rediscounting paper; the other with redepositing of funds. It will be recalled that the Bank has authority to rediscount paper for state banks that make of it a legal depositary. Thus while the law restricts the Bank from loaning to private individuals or corporations except on certain warehouse receipts and real estate security, it may, nevertheless, indirectly loan to private individuals and corporations in amounts and against collateral that needs only to meet with the approval of the Industrial Commission.

In a bank possessed of so large a volume of public funds on deposit, the question of the manner of redepositing a part of them is an important one. It is particularly important when those deposits are drawn from widely scattered communities, and branch-banking is not developed. But the legislature evaded answering the question with specific directions, and in the lone sentence of Section 14 gave the Industrial Commission the power to determine the terms and conditions of redepositing its public and private funds. The lack of any definite restrictions and directions concerning the rediscounting of paper and the redepositing of funds explains in large part much of the corruption and mismanagement of the Bank for the purpose of acquiring political ends. Bank officials might redeposit all of the public funds of the state with a single bank and demand no interest and still be strictly within the law. The corruption and misuse of public funds in connection with the Scandinavian American Bank of Fargo (of which Nonpartisan and Independent are alike ashamed) would have been impossible had the ordinary restrictions and limitations on a bank's management been placed in the law.

BANK EXAMINATION

The state examiner, or his deputies, is directed to examine the Bank of North Dakota at least twice a year. He is to examine the assets with a view to determining whether they are correctly valued on the Bank's books. He is to investigate the Bank's methods of operation and accounting. His report is to be made to the Industrial Commission, to the next legislative assembly, and to the State Banking Board.[1]

CRITICISM

Thus did the legislators make provision for a State Bank. The kindest criticism that can be made is to say that the Bank Act was well-intentioned. No one can but admire the legislators for their desire to create an institution designed to bring relief and prosperity to the mass of citizens within the state. The legislators deserve hearty praise for their desire to put public moneys held by public treasurers to work for the people of the state. But the Bank Act that they drafted to create such an institution is a mischievous piece of legislation. It is not worthy of the cause it is designed to advance. It represents one of the biggest blunders that the Nonpartisans can be held responsible for. It is a monument to the recklessness of its authors, if not of their ignorance of sound banking principles. No prudent legislator would have granted such sweeping powers to a politically

[1] *Session Laws of 1919*, chap. 147, sec. 23.

elective body like the Industrial Commission. Even though the greatest faith were had in both the honesty and ability of the immediate members of the Commission, the risk would be great that political opponents capture the seats of authority and use their power to destroy what the legislator would have built. No judicious legislators would have approved of an act so meager in its specifications of the manner in which the Bank should be operated. The danger of incompetence, rashness, or political bias is always present in an administrative body. Legislators cannot be too careful in framing laws to make them sufficiently specific so that the intent of the law cannot be warped and twisted by administrators, until the original design of the law is completely lost. Unfortunately, the Act creating the Bank of North Dakota was so drafted as to permit a politically elective body to determine its course.

It sometimes happens that a very bad law may be so intelligently and ably administered that a large part of the mischief that might have been done under its administration will be averted. The hope of the Bank of North Dakota lay in an intelligent, fearless, nonpartisan administration of the Bank by the Industrial Commission. Its parent, the law, was impotent once the Bank was born. Its organization and career were determined by the Industrial Commission. The history of the Bank from this point on becomes largely a tale of the Industrial Commission's maneuvers in its attempts to operate the Bank in such a manner as it should "deem most fit to promote the efficiency of the public service."

CHAPTER IV

Relation of the Bank of North Dakota to the Existing Banking Systems

THE FOUNDERS' VIEWS OF THE BANK'S POSITION

The preceding chapter aimed to present the salient features of the laws creating the Bank of North Dakota and providing for its organization and operation. It was hoped that thereby the reader would be able to form a picture of the institution provided for by law. The Bank was created to operate in a commonwealth already possessing both state and national banking systems. It is the purpose of this chapter to show (1) what place the founders expected the Bank to occupy in the existing credit structure; (2) how local banks were compelled to recognize its dominant position; and (3) the manner in which the Bank rendered banking service.

In his message to the 1919 legislative assembly Governor Frazier expressed himself as follows: "I recommend the establishment of a State Bank which will act in a similar capacity for our state as does the Federal Reserve and Farm Land Banks for the district in which they are located." [1] Of course, this statement was made before the Bank Act was drafted. It is of special significance, however, because it fell from the lips of one who, because of his dominant position on the Industrial Commission, was to have the main voice in the operation of the Bank. During

[1] *Journal of the House of the Sixteenth Session of the Legislative Assembly*, p. 20.

the time in which the Bank was being organized, but before it opened for business, the following official statement was made: "The policy of the Bank of North Dakota is . . . to be helpful to and to assist in the development of the State and National Banks and other financial institutions and public corporations within the state and not, in any manner, to destroy or to be harmful to existing financial institutions." [1]

In statements issued by the director general there is further evidence of the Bank's policy toward existing financial institutions. In answer to the question, "Will you do commercial banking?", the answer is given:

No, not in the ordinary acceptance of the term "commercial banking". Individuals, associations, or private corporations are not permitted under the law, to borrow money on unsecured notes, or on notes secured by chattel mortgages or collateral, or on any other class of personal security, except warehouse receipts, (real estate loans, however, may be accepted; also loans secured by State or Government obligations).[2]

In answer to the question, "Will you receive individual deposits?", the director general replies:

No, not from residents of the State of North Dakota. Deposits of individuals, firms, and private corporations in the State, should be made in the established other financial institutions. In as much as the Bank of North Dakota cannot make loans to individuals, associations or private corporations (except as herein-before indicated) it does not propose to withdraw private funds from the localities where such loans ought to be made. Individual deposits from outside the State will be welcomed, thereby increasing the ability of the Bank

[1] Order no. 1, issued May 12, 1919.

[2] Circular no. 2, series of 1920.

of North Dakota to meet the requirements of such localities as may need additional funds.[1]

The founders of the Bank of North Dakota did not establish regular branches, but sought to establish a relationship with the then existing state and natonal banks in which the new institution would be a central bank and its position somewhat similar to that of federal reserve banks to their members. Part of its policy was "To mobilize the assets of the whole state and its entire financial worth into one large central bank cooperating with all the banks in the state." [2] It sought to do this in the following manner. It invited the existing state and national banks to carry balances with the Bank. They were encouraged in this by the provision in the Bank Act which allowed such balances to be considered "available funds". At the same time the Bank officials urged the state and national banks to use their good judgment in determining what part of their reserves they would shift from their present correspondents to the Bank of North Dakota.[3] Suggestion was made that the size of the balance carried with the Bank of North Dakota ought to bear some close proportion "to the discount or other facilities that would be asked for by the depositary bank, and should be along the line of such reciprocal relations as would best conserve the financial interests of the whole state and of all its financial institutions." [4]

STATE CLEARING HOUSE CREATED

The Bank of North Dakota was intended to function as a State Clearing House, and a par collection system among state banks of North Dakota was provided for in Section

[1] Circular no. 2, series of 1920.

[2] Order no. 1, series 1920, issued May 12, 1919.

[3] Order no. 6, series 1920, issued July 3, 1919.

[4] *Ibid.*

13 of the Act. This was to be similar to that which the Federal Reserve System established for the nation, but the punishment for refusal to remit at par was somewhat more severe (guilty of misdemeanor).

REDEPOSIT POLICY

Finally, the redeposit policy evolved by the first Industrial Commission indicates what position the Bank was to have among the existing banks. The Bank Act placed the responsibility of creating a redeposit policy upon the shoulders of the Industrial Commission which, since the Act made neither suggestions nor restrictions, had a free hand in the matter. The Industrial Commission deserves credit for having decided upon a policy that seems highly commendable. The essence of this policy was that redeposits should be made so as to leave the public funds pretty much where they would have been in the absence of the Bank of North Dakota. We will have occasion to explain this policy in greater detail in the next chapter. It is sufficient here to show that the founders of the Bank had no desire to draw the funds out of the existing banking system and into the new state institution.

SUMMARY

To sum up; the Bank's relation to the existing credit structure was to be similar to that of a federal reserve bank to the member banks in its district. It was to do a very limited business aside from that conducted with banks; the reserves of the state were to be concentrated in it; it was to be the center of a par clearing and collection system; it was to furnish its credit to the public primarily through the medium of the local banks which would rediscount with the Central Bank; it was to be intimately connected with the fiscal operations of the state, for it would have charge of the sale of state securities and would be the sole legal depositary of all public funds. In one respect it was to go further, "It was to meet the needs for and to perform the functions of a joint stock land bank." [1]

METHOD OF GAINING COOPERATION OF STATE BANKS

The founders of the Bank of North Dakota employed tactics not unlike those of the Federal Reserve Board to gain the cooperation of the existing state and national banks. That is to say, the Bank Act and subsequent rulings and orders of the Bank officials and Industrial Commission made the position of any bank which assumed an unfriendly attitude very uncomfortable. In one sense the method of compelling national banks to come into the Federal Reserve System was more drastic for if they refused they lost their charters. In another sense the method of compulsion was not less drastic in North Dakota. It is true that both the law and the avowed policy of the Bank left the question of joining the system a matter of voluntary decision on the part of the local state and national banks. But as a matter of fact to refuse to join was to forego the privilege of being used as a depositary bank by the Bank of North Dakota. This would have been a hard blow to most North Dakota banks. The country is new; capital is scarce; individual deposits run relatively light, and the public funds which heretofore had been an important and reliable source of funds to the local banks would now be transferred to the Bank of North Dakota. Furthermore, any bank designated as a depositary bank that did not carry part of its reserve funds with the Bank of North Dakota was not permitted to rediscount.[2] Thus a bank refusing to cooperate with the Bank of North Dakota would be compelled to forego the privilege of having a central bank where, when necessity

[1] Order no. 1, series 1920, issued May 12, 1919.

[2] Rule 1 to banks, sec. 12.

arose, it could liquidate some of its paper. Such a bank would be caught by both jaws of the vise. If it refused to join, its public deposits would be withdrawn and its paper would be less liquid. In consequence the inducement to state banks to deposit a part of their reserve in the Bank of North Dakota was very strong, particularly when, as is so often the case with small country banks, they did not enjoy good connections with large banks outside the state. To such banks the matter of joining as a " member " of the Bank of North Dakota virtually became a necessity, and many came into the system.

METHOD OF SUPPLYING CREDIT

The Bank of North Dakota supplied credit directly or indirectly in several different ways. Its constant endeavor was to deal directly with local banks only. The bank officials advised the farmers who sought credit of the type which the law authorized them to grant to individuals directly, to go to their local banks and let these act as agents for them. For instance, the law states that the Bank of North Dakota " may make loans to any individual, association, or private corporation secured by duly recorded first mortgage on real estate in the state of North Dakota . . . or secured by warehouse receipts issued by the Industrial Commission or by any licensed warehouse within the state." The Bank, however, " strongly recommended " that individuals desiring a real estate loan appoint a local bank as agent in securing the loan. By so doing, friendly relations would be engendered between farmer and local banker.[1] It was pointed out that " it would not be good business judgment [for the borrower] to cut himself entirely loose

[1] *The Bank of North Dakota,* an official compilation of Laws, Regulations, By-Laws, etc., published by the Bank of North Dakota, 1920, p. 43.

[2] Circular no. 5, series of 1920, issued February 2, 1920.

from connections with his local banker,"[2] for "the local bank is usually in a good position to assist the borrower in meeting his annual installment payments promptly on the day they come due and can make such temporary advances pending threshing or other seasonal delays, as may be required by the borrower for that purpose."[1] The Bank did not press the matter further than to make this urgent recommendation to prospective borrowers. Many local banks sought appointments as agents, but were refused, as the matter was held to be "entirely optional with the borrower".[2]

LOANS MADE

An examination of the resources as listed in monthly bank statements of the Bank of North Dakota and published in its bulletin reveals that it loaned funds as follows:

1. To local banks within the state;
2. To individuals presenting warehouse receipts as collateral;
3. To individuals on real estate mortgages;
4. To public institutions and departments.

In the chapter above the legal authority for making these loans was presented. It remains for us here to set forth the manner in which the Industrial Commission undertook to carry out the legal provisions.

BANK LOAN POLICY

Under the title "loans to banks" we will consider not only the money loaned on the local bank's own note, but also the money received by the local bank when rediscounting paper taken from its portfolio. These two methods of lending have been, for the most part, treated together in the Act and the published Bank statements do not differentiate between them.

[1] *The Bank of North Dakota*, p. 43.

[2] Circular no. 4, series of 1920, issued February 2, 1920.

It will be recalled that the Act permits the Bank to rediscount paper for depositary banks, and to make loans to local banks upon terms and under conditions determined by the Industrial Commission. One of the first rules that the Industrial Commission formulated was that banks wishing to avail themselves of the privileges of rediscounting with, or borrowing from the Bank of North Dakota must file a certified copy of a resolution adopted by the local bank's board of directors indicating that certain officers of the local bank had authority to rediscount with the Bank of North Dakota any notes in the bank's portfolio, or to borrow from the Bank of North Dakota and offer as security for the loan any of the assets of the bank that are customarily hypothecated.[1] In the same rule, paper eligible for rediscount was described as follows:

> Notes offered to the Bank of North Dakota for rediscount shall be of not more than six months' maturity; shall be negotiable in form; shall be accompanied by certificate copy of chattel mortgage, duly filed, which chattel mortgage shall be a first mortgage on the property described therein; and the note shall be accompanied by a copy of the financial statement of the borrower on file with the rediscounting bank.[2]

Further on in the same communication are other minor rules. Thus the rediscounting bank is required to endorse without restriction its rediscount offerings in order that it may guarantee the payment of the rediscounted note at maturity.[3] The rediscounting bank is required to have sufficient funds to cover the rediscounted note on deposit with the Bank of North Dakota at the date of its maturity.[4]

[1] Rule 1, series of 1920, no. 6.

[2] *Ibid.*, no. 7.

[3] *Ibid.*, no. 8.

[4] *Ibid.*, no. 9.

Rediscounted notes cannot be renewed. If a local bank be hard pressed it must present other notes for rediscount.[1] Rediscounted notes may be sent to the rediscounting member bank for collection, but remain the property of the Bank of North Dakota until the note has been charged to the bank's account with the State Bank.[2]

WAREHOUSE RECEIPT LOAN POLICY

The Bank Act makes more specific provisions concerning the making of loans on warehouse receipts. It will be recalled that only such warehouse receipts were acceptable as were issued by the Industrial Commission or by licensed warehouses. Furthermore, the law specified that the loan might not exceed ninety per cent of the value of the commodity evidenced by the warehouse receipt. These restrictions seemed too drastic to the members of the Industrial Commission and they soon went on record as favoring additional legislation which would permit the Bank to loan directly on grain stored in the farmer's granary. Meanwhile they urged local banks to make such grain loans and to rediscount such paper at the Bank.[3] Thus they hoped to be of indirect assistance in loaning funds on grain stored on the farm.

REAL ESTATE LOAN POLICY

The Industrial Commission worked out the following plan for making loans on real estate mortgages. In the beginning only applications for loans on farm lands would be considered. Ranch land and city real estate could not, for the time being, be used as security for a loan. Loans would be made for thirty years. A plan was worked out whereby the borrower was to pay seven per cent of the orig-

[1] Rule 1, series of 1920, no. 10.

[2] *Ibid.*, no. 11.

[3] Circular no. 6, series of 1920, issued February 2, 1920.

inal amount of the loan annually. This amount would not only cover the interest charge (six per cent) on the unpaid principal, but would entirely amortize the loan in thirty-four years. Any installments remaining unpaid at the end of the thirtieth year were to be paid at that time in order that the loan might then be retired. This awkward amortization plan was resorted to because the Bank officials were unwilling to fix a rate higher than seven per cent *per annum* on the original amount of the loan, and the law required that the loan run not more than thirty years. Installment payments might be made in advance, but would not be permitted to be in arrears except as provided by law in case of crop failure. Eight per cent interest would be charged on deferred installment payments. The Bank would regard with favor applications for loans on improved farms, and especially if the owner lived on the land and carried on diversified farming. The Bank would not favor granting loans on land without buildings when the owner had unencumbered land with buildings, for the Bank would demand the best security the borrower had to offer. The amount of the loan that the Bank would make could in no case exceed fifty per cent of the value of the property mortgaged. In case the buildings were not in an excellent state of repair or did not represent an adequate and proportional equipment, the amount of the loan might not exceed fifty per cent of the land value plus thirty per cent of the value of the buildings.[1]

These were the main features of the Industrial Commission's plan for the Bank's mortgage-loan business. Minor rules concerning insurance, papers, conveying title, fees, etc. are to be found, but they are neither novel nor of fundamental importance.

[1] The above paragraph is based on rule 3, series of 1920.

PUBLIC INSTITUTIONS' AND DEPARTMENTS' LOAN POLICY

Section 15 of the Bank Act provided that funds of the Bank could be transferred " to other departments, institutions, utilities, industries, enterprises or business projects of the state, which [should] be returned with interest to the Bank." Apparently the Industrial Commission never formulated a definite policy with respect to these loans, or at all events never published it. However, material that sheds some light on this question may be found in the Industrial Commission's report for the year 1920. In explaining the overdrafts shown on the financial statements of the Mill and Elevator Association, the report says:

In order that the Commission might at all times know the amounts that were being expended in construction of the Grand Forks project, it was deemed advisable to carry the checks drawn by the Grand Forks, Fargo and Drake businesses as overdrafts and to have the Industrial Commission thereby be kept informed as to the amounts being invested at Grand Forks. Then at the end of different periods the Commission would authorize transfers and the execution of notes therefor. Since Dec. 31st the Commission has authorized a transfer to the Mill and Elevator Association and such transfer has been made and note executed to the Bank of North Dakota for the sum of $200,000 to take care of the overdraft shown in this exhibit.[1]

The following comment on the overdraft of the Home Builders Association account is found in the same report:

The reason for its existence and the manner of its handling is the same as is discussed concerning the overdraft of the mill and elevator association in the commentary following Exhibit II. Since Dec. 31st the Industrial Commission has

[1] *Financial Report of the North Dakota Industrial Program for the Period ending December 31, 1920*, p. 6.

authorized the transfer of funds in the amount of $60,000 to the House Builders Association, which transfer has taken up this overdraft.[1]

The manner of taking up these overdrafts was as follows. The Industrial Commission would adopt a resolution authorizing and directing the Bank of North Dakota to advance and loan a specified amount to the industry or enterprise and receive for it a note payable on demand and bearing six per cent interest *per annum*.[2]

Nothing has been found that would indicate that the loans made to educational, penal, and industrial institutions to carry them over the period pending tax collections were unusual in their form. It is fair to assume that they were made on the strength of unsecured demand notes and bore six per cent interest *per annum*.

[1] *Financial Report, op. cit.*, p. 22.

[2] *House Journal of the Seventeenth Legislative Assembly* (hereafter referred to as *House Journal*, 1921), pp. 215, 289, 291, 292, 293.

CHAPTER V

Operation of the Bank of North Dakota from the Time of its Organization to November 2, 1920

ORGANIZATION AND PREPARATION

The Industrial Commission met on April 4, 1919, selected temporary quarters for the Bank, and appointed J. R. Waters to be its manager. On April 9, 1919, F. W. Cathro was appointed director general of the Bank. The work of organization then went on during the early summer. Rules, regulations and orders were issued from time to time by the Industrial Commission and the director general of the Bank.

The organization of the Bank was somewhat as follows: The manager was the general agent of the Industrial Commission. His duties were to approve the purchase of office equipment, to approve appointments and employ and dismiss Bank employees, to approve surety bonds of national banks wishing to become depositary banks, and to keep in his custody the completed real-estate notes and mortgages until they were delivered to the state treasurer to become the basis for a state bond issue.[1] Subordinate to the manager was the director general. To him was given "direct supervision of all the departments of the Bank, except as set forth in the duties of the Manager."[2] He was to direct the assignment of work in the several departments, to pass "upon the decisions of the several heads of

[1] *The Bank of North Dakota*, p. 23. This is Regulation "C" adopted by the Industrial Commission May 8, 1919.

[2] *Ibid.*

the departments . . . with the power of veto,"[1] to direct the "disbursement of funds in the custody of the Bank,"[2] and to authorize "the expenditure of funds for the use of the Bank, except as provided in the duties of the Manager."[3]

Five coordinate departments were created in the Bank, namely, the bond, farm loan, credits, audits, and statistics and publicity departments. A department director was put in immediate charge of each.[4] A legal department was also established, and a transit department under the audits department.[5] The department directors were charged with duties appropriate to their office, a detailed list of which would be too long to present here. The five department directors together with the director general were to constitute the "General Finance Committee". The director general was designated as chairman of this committee which was ordered to meet daily at ten o'clock to "confer and advise with the director general".[6]

PUBLIC FUNDS ORDERED TRANSFERRED

A most important order was issued on July 7, 1919, by Director General Cathro. The treasurers of all political subdivisions, state, county, township, municipal and school districts, as well as all public institutions, were ordered, pursuant to bank law, to deposit in the Bank of North Dakota all funds which they had under their care. The following schedule was to be observed in depositing public funds. On July 28 all public corporations (townships, mu-

[1] *The Bank of North Dakota, op. cit.*

[2] *Ibid.*

[3] *Ibid.*

[4] *Ibid.*

[5] *Ibid.*, also *The Bank of North Dakota*, pp. 49-50.

[6] *Ibid.*

nicipalities and school districts) in the first judicial district were to deposit their funds. Similar deposits were to be made on July 29 from the second judicial district, on July 30 from the third judicial district, on July 31 from the fourth judicial district, on August 1 from the fifth judicial district, on August 2 from the sixth judicial district, on August 4 from the seventh judicial district, on August 5 from the eighth judicial district, on August 6 from the ninth judicial district, on August 7 from the tenth judicial district, on August 8 from the eleventh judicial district, and on August 9 from the twelfth judicial district. On August 11 all county funds of all counties throughout the state under the control of county treasurers were to be deposited. On August 14 all state funds under the control of the state treasurer were to be deposited. On August 18 all funds of all penal, educational and industrial institutions, excepting those under the control of the state treasurer, were to be deposited. On August 21 all other public funds of whatever kind were to be deposited.

In case public funds were loaned out under contract entered into prior to February 25, 1919, they were to be transferred to the Bank of North Dakota only upon the termination of such contract, or indeed they were not required to be turned over until two months after the contract had expired.

The manner in which the public funds were to be transferred from the local banks to the Bank of North Dakota was set forth in Rule 2.[1] The treasurer of each public corporation was to draw checks for the balance on deposit in each bank in which he carried public funds subject to check. These checks were to be mailed to the audit department of the Bank of North Dakota for credit. However, it was

[1] *The Bank of North Dakota*, p. 37.

not the intention of the Bank to draw all of the public funds into Bismarck. As soon as a treasurer drew a check on a local bank and sent it to the Bank of North Dakota for deposit, the check was to be redeposited in the bank on which it was drawn, provided that such bank was eligible as a depositary bank.[1] The object in so redepositing public funds was to disturb as little as possible the financial arrangements throughout the state and work as little hardship as possible on the banks which held public deposits at the time.

THE BANK OPENS FOR BUSINESS

The bank bonds having been delivered to the Industrial Commission, the Bank was legally opened for business July 28, 1919. In accordance with the director general's order the public treasurers began to deposit public funds in the Bank on the day it was opened, and these deposits grew from day to day as the public treasurers of the various districts complied with the order of the Bank official. It will be observed that the Bank as yet had no capital. On July 31, 1919, a cashier's check was drawn on the Bank of North Dakota in favor of the Industrial Commission for $500,000 in payment of Nos. M1–M500 five per cent bonds, Bank Series. This check was endorsed by the Industrial Commission as follows: "Pay to the Bank of North Dakota", and was stamped "paid" August 1, 1919. The Bank therefore had purchased $500,000 worth of bonds and on August 1, 1919 had received $500,000 capital in the form of the endorsed cashier's check. A similar cashier's check was drawn on August 4, 1919, this time, however, for $1,500,000 and in payment for five per cent bonds, Bank Series, Nos. M501 to M1000, $500,000; D1 to D1000, $500,000; C1 to C4000, $400,000; 1–2000, $100,000. This check was endorsed in effect like the first and stamped

[1] *The Bank of North Dakota*, p. 51.

"paid" August 4, 1919. The Bank now had bought the entire issue of bank bonds, had paid for them by drawing two cashier's checks on the public funds deposited with it and had received as its capital these same checks endorsed by the Industrial Commission. Consequently in receiving its capital the Bank received not a dollar of actual money, but in effect the $2,000,000 issue of bank bonds.

VOLUME OF BUSINESS

A fortnight after the Bank opened for business the first public statement was issued in the Bank bulletin. The statement showed the condition of the Bank as of August 15, 1919. According to this statement $4,110,556.51 had been deposited by 2,073 public corporations. The table printed herewith shows that this sum steadily grew until it had reached its highest point in April, 1920, when the statement for April 15 shows public deposits of $28,734,241.83. Thereafter public deposits steadily fell off until the statement of October 16 shows $14,531,143.00.

Total Public Deposits with the Bank of North Dakota as of the 15, 16 or 17 of the Month

August, 1919	$4,110,556.51
September	8,717,570.30
October	9,185,241.55
November	9,694,239.93
December	9,325,837.32
January, 1920	13,579,471.70
February	15,507,915.69
March	25,295,479.40
April	28,734,241.83
May	23,012,964.94
June	20,246,238.17
July	17,315,485.01
August	15,358,923.46
September	14,487,121.05
October	14,153,143.00

The local banks that affiliated with the Bank of North

Dakota as member banks constituted another important source of deposits. On August 15, 1919 it appears that 396 banks of the state had opened accounts with the Bank of North Dakota and carried balances totaling $1,425,528.26.[1] Doubtless these accounts were opened with the Bank of North Dakota in order that the local banks might continue to share in the use of public deposits, as well as to avail themselves of rediscounting privileges, and to share in the advantages of the new par collection system.

It was with this equipment of capital, deposits from local banks and public corporations, and membership of state banks that the Bank undertook to render the service for which it was designed. Total resources were given as $7,883,558.76.[2]

STATE CLEARINGS

There seems to have been a considerable agitation on the part of North Dakota bankers for some sort of state clearing house that would facilitate the collection of checks throughout the state.[3] So it is not surprising that this service was developed notably from the first. The Bank had been open to the public only a month when the average daily state clearings were $755,950.30 and the average daily clearings of all items both domestic and foreign were $1,042,960.48. These figures grew somewhat during the following month, and for the month ending November 15 the domestic clearings had practically reached the million-dollar-a-day mark. At the same time average total clearings were more than a million and a quarter dollars a day, constituting an average of 6,568 items.[4] At the end of 1920 the Industrial

[1] *Bank of North Dakota Bulletin*, August, 1919.

[2] *Ibid.*, August, 1919.

[3] *Ibid.*, January, 1920.

[4] *Ibid.*, November, 1919.

Commission was able to report that the Bank of North Dakota was doing business with about eight-ninths of the banks in the state, and that the Bank was serving as "a clearing house for a large percentage of all the transit items cleared in the state." The average daily clearings for the first year were given as approximately $800,000.[1] This mass of items was handled by the Bank without making any collection charges against its depositary banks. Practically all points throughout the state were made par collection points.

REDEPOSITS

When the public treasurers sent to the Bank of North Dakota drafts drawn on the banks where public funds were on deposit it immediately redeposited them in the banks on which they were drawn. Thus the necessary transfer of public funds could be made without any shifting of funds or inconvenient calling of loans. Thereafter, however, the proceeds of tax collections could lawfully be deposited only in the Bank of North Dakota. In the distribution of these deposits the Bank substantially followed the plan of redepositing the funds in the communities where they originated. Exceptions might be made in cases where a wealthy community could well afford to forego the redeposits in order that they might be placed in poorer communities which needed more banking funds.[2] The manner in which these funds were redeposited has been the cause of much bitter criticism of the Bank officials then in power. For it was discovered that these redeposits were sometimes made with flagrant disregard of the principles already stated. While most people would have agreed that in exceptional cases there was good reason to favor poorer communities at

[1] *Financial Report of the North Dakota Industrial Program* for the year ending December 31, 1920, pp. 21, 22.

[2] *House Journal*, 1921, pp. 216-217.

the expense of the wealthier, still it was hard to see why, for instance, Cass county, said to be the richest in the state, should receive more in redeposits than the amount of public deposits carried with the Bank of North Dakota by the public treasurers of the county. Figures were made public showing that on January 19, 1921 the treasurers in Cass county had $330,988.16 on deposit in the Bank of North Dakota.[1] At the same time the Bank had redeposited $434,206.31 within the county.[2] Here was a surplus of $103,218.15 in redeposits coming from the poorer counties to the wealthiest one of the state. Moreover local banks in Cass county had loans and rediscounts to the amount of $181,189.81 on the same date.[3] Thus an excess of $284,-407.96 over and above the amount due to treasurers within Cass county had been returned to local bankers therein. Surely here was a manifest violation of the principle to re-deposit funds in the locality in which they originated, or in exceptional cases to favor poorer counties at the expense of the wealthier ones. More amazing still is the fact that the greater part of these funds were placed in but one of the thirty-five depositary banks in the county. The Scandinavian American Bank of Fargo had received $229,883.05 in redeposits, and $175,189.81 in loans and rediscounts![4]

THE SCANDINAVIAN AMERICAN BANK OF FARGO

A history of the Bank of North Dakota during the years 1919 and 1920 cannot be written without very definite reference to the Scandinavian American Bank of Fargo. The Scandinavian American Bank was a state bank capitalized at $50,000 and possessed of a $10,000 surplus. It was purchased in 1917 bv League leaders because they believed

[1] *House Journal*, 1921, p. 597.

[2] *Ibid.*, p. 597.

[3] *Ibid.*, p. 597.

[4] *Ibid.*, p. 596.

that the League needed a financial institution to finance its paper.[1]

The Nonpartisan League received its financial support mainly through farmers' notes (accommodation paper) and by the membership dues. The latter were frequently paid with post-dated checks. Either of these resources had to be placed with some banking institution before actual funds would be available. The Scandinavian American Bank was the first of what was to have been a series of banks throughout the state which were to serve the League in the negotiation of these types of paper peculiar to the League and the farmers.[2] However, the needs of the League, the needs of the League institutions, and the cupidity of some of its leaders grew far too fast for this expanding banking system. The result was that the Scandinavian American Bank was flooded with the paper of the League, its pet enterprises and their promoters.

The manner in which the League leaders acquired the Scandinavian American Bank is little less remarkable than the manner in which they abused the bank later on. According to testimony before the House Committee the League got control of the Scandinavian American Bank by purchasing a controlling amount of stock with funds borrowed from the Exchange National Bank of St. Paul which took as collateral for the loan the stock purchased with the proceeds of the loan. Somewhat later the Exchange National Bank called this loan and arrangements were made whereby the Mercantile State Bank of Minneapolis took it over on the same collateral.[3] Later still the loan was transferred somewhere in North Dakota. The League thus be-

[1] *House Journal*, 1921, pp. 255-256. It is said to have been purchased by Mr. Hastings on instructions from Messrs. Townley and Lemke

[2] *Ibid.*, p. 581.

[3] It is said that the Bank of North Dakota redeposited funds with the Mercantile State Bank of Minneapolis as a reward for making this loan. *House Journal*, 1921, p. 274.

came the owner of a controlling amount of the stock of the Scandinavian American Bank through funds borrowed on the strength of the stock itself.[1]

Even before the Scandinavian American Bank was taken over by the promoters of the League its strength had not been unquestioned. But after the League's leaders were in charge the bank's portfolio contained more and more questionable paper. By April, 1918 its position was such as to call forth the "shoot it to other banks" letter, upon the occasion of the Guaranty Fund Commission's examination.[2] "In April, 1919 Deputy Examiner, P. E. Hall-

[1] *House Journal*, 1921, pp. 275, 350.

[2] Office of State Examiner State of North Dakota
Bismarck, N. D.,
June 10, 1918.

Mr. J. J. Hastings, Vice President,
Scandinavian American Bank,
Fargo, N. D.

Dear Mr. Hastings:—

Mr. Waters submitted to an operation at the hospital here today. While the operation is not serious yet he is not very well and will be laid up for a while. This is the reason that you and Mr. Semington were not able to get him over the phone.

He has asked me to write you regarding the extra help you have at your bank just now making an examination. He has been sick since last Thursday, or he would have headed the thing off. Being that Mr. Schroegge, Mr. Semington, and Mr. Halldorson are there now to make an examination on behalf of the commission, he does not care to create any animosity and antagonism over this matter at this time, and get as good a report for them as possible, so that they won't have anything to hand the opposition parties over league finances and business methods, or criticize the amount of paper carried there. It appears quite evident that this is a political play for thunder. You see the opposition parties are a little short on real sensational thunder, and they are trying to scare up something for the last act, and I don't suppose the other banks in Fargo are just what you would term "crazy about you." Mr. Waters wishes me to advise that if the examiners object to any of the paper carried there, you are to tell them that it will be removed at once. The plan for taking care of objectionable matter is to shoot it out to the other league banks—Grand Forks, Hillsboro, Buxton, Hatton—these banks are practically all new banks, and have been passed by the commission which will leave them in a position to do this. They would not have anything that the Commission would object to just now.

dorson, made an examination of the Scandinavian American Bank and reported its condition as serious, its loans as excessive, and its connection with the League enterprises as intimate." [1] Early in September, Halldorson made another examination of the bank, and in a report submitted to the State Banking Board dated September 17, and showing the condition of the bank as of September 6, he again called attention to excessive loans and deficient collateral.[2]

In the report Mr. Halldorson showed, among other things, that excessive loans had been made to individual borrowers. The Scandinavian American Bank's capital and surplus amounted to $60,000. This would have permitted it, under North Dakota banking laws, to make loans of not more than $9,000 to any individual, concern, or corporation.[3] As a matter of fact Halldorson's report disclosed the following excessive loans:

United Consumers Stores Company	$194,675.71
Nonpartisan or N. P. League	129,148.55
League Exchange	66,182.24
Publishers National Service Bureau	47,952.06
U. S. Sisal Trust	12,000.00
Danielson Brothers	22,782.16
A. M. Grosvenor	18,066.33
The Haggarty line	47,088.00
The Porter Kimball line	15,082.45
The Knack line	23,000.00
P. C. Johnke	9,538.89

Anything that you sent them could be taken back later if necessary. Of course, we don't want to move any more than is absolutely necessary, to get by with a clean report. Mr. Waters is satisfied that with this information, you and Mr. Semington will be able to handle this matter satisfactorily to all.

If anything further develops, kindly write me.

Very truly yours,

Roy M. Halliday

Langer, William, *The Nonpartisan League*, p. 79.

[1] *House Journal*, 1921, p. 162.

[2] *Ibid.*, p. 162.

[3] *Compiled Laws of North Dakota*, 1913, Civil Code, chap. 28, sec. 5172.

Besides those listed above there were others, so that the total amount in excessive loans was $683,290.85, which was considerably over fifty per cent of the $1,144,910.15 of loans and discounts that the bank then had.[1] Mr. Halldorson described the general character of the loans as being " very poor ", and made mention of the fact that the bank's paper was worse than it had appeared in April, the total of past due paper having nearly reached the $200,000 mark.[2]

On September 27 following, Halldorson accompanied by Mr. A. E. Sheets of the attorney general's office, began a supplementary examination of the bank and on October 1 made a report [3] in which it was stated that there now appeared to be excessive loans to the total amount of $734,000, whose general character was extremely unsatisfactory, and whose security was generally inadequate.[4] The report described several of the loans listed in the excessive loans list, and these descriptions reveal the methods by which the recipients of the excessive loans circumvented the law. The method was to get a number of individuals associated with the concern to make out individual notes. The Consumers United Stores Company's line of credit is typical. This line aggregated $170,000 at the time of the October examination. The following excerpt from Halldorson's report read into the records at the hearings of the Audit Committee of the house of representatives gives a good description of the manner in which so much money was secured for one concern and the type of security held for the loan.

The Consumers United Stores Company has a line of credit extended through a system of individual loans to twenty-three individuals, aggregating in all $170,000. The individual paper

[1] *House Journal*, 1921, p. 345.

[2] *Ibid.*, p. 162.

[3] *Fargo Courier-News*, October 3, 1919.

[4] *North Dakota Reports*, vol. 46, p. 468.

is given for accommodation purposes only, and is secured by notes representing farmers' liabilities in the sum of $100 to $50, together with post-dated checks of $32 and less, amounting in all to $554,364.88. It should be here noted that it was impossible to make an examination or even check this vast amount of collateral, and that the figures in the bank have been taken for the purpose of this as correct. It should also be noted, however, that $291,435.55 of the amount of the above notes and post-dated checks are not now in the bank, but are in the hands of the Consumers United Stores Company for the purpose of collection. All that the bank has to show for this amount of collateral out for collection is receipts for the same, signed by the officers and employees of the Consumers United Stores Company. It is estimated that the farmers' notes held as collateral are not worth in excess of fifty per cent of their par value. This is a liberal statement as to this class of collateral hypothecated for the loans under discussion.

The post dated checks are held as a portion of the collateral for this loan, and since they are held as collateral for the second largest loan made by the bank, require some explanation. These post dated checks are in the sum of $32 and are payable at future dates. It is our opinion that these checks are not in law or in fact collateral at all. A current dated check, in itself, is not collateral, and a post dated check would be for the same reason of a smaller value for similar purposes, for the purpose of collateral and security for loans. It is our opinion that post dated checks are without any validity or substantial value.[1]

The National Nonpartisan League obtained its loan in a similar manner. Halldorson's criticism of this loan was as follows:

The National Nonpartisan League line of credit consists of twenty-two individual notes ranging in different amounts from $840 to $8,000, and aggregating in all $148,824.26. A consid-

[1] *House Journal*, 1921, p. 318.

eration of the names of the makers of these accommodation notes will illustrate that the same condition attends the extension of this line as has formerly been explained in the line of credit extended to the Consumers United Stores Company. The individual notes represent only accommodation paper. The individual notes represent a single line and are so considered by the bank. The security held by the bank as collateral for its loans made to the Nonpartisan League for $148,824.26 consists principally of post dated checks in the sum of $274,-864.01. As to the value of this class of collateral reference is here made to the discussion and opinion of the same made above, and which is now made a part hereof.

There is also fifty-seven shares of the Peoples State Bank of Hatton bank stock with an estimated market value of $115 each amounting in total to $6,555, held by the bank as security for this line of credit. Discussion of the value of this class of collateral will be made hereafter.

In addition to this Consumers United Stores Company bonds in the sum of $20,000 is held as collateral. It is our opinion from an examination of these bonds that they represent nothing more than individual liability of the Consumers United Stores Company, a corporation. These bonds represent collateral already discussed in the form of farmers notes as security for the United Consumers Stores line of credit and constitute a pyramiding of that collateral. In fact, they amount to nothing more than the signature of the Consumers Stores Company to the indebtedness which they secure.[1]

Finally Halldorson's comments on the loan to the League Exchange are interesting because of the bank-stock collateral offered. It will be seen that the entire holdings of Scandinavian American Bank stock were offered as collateral by the League Exchange for a loan from the Scandinavian American Bank, and were so accepted by that institution.

[1] *House Journal*, 1921, p. 319.

This line consists of $66,182.21, and comprises nine notes ranging from $2,149.34 to $9,000, aggregating that total. The security which the bank holds for this advancement comprises farmers' notes of the kind previously described, with a par value of $20,181.58; also bank stock of the following banks: Security State Bank of Courtenay, ten shares, market value $1,200; Peoples State Bank of Hillsboro, ten shares, market value, $1,200; Scandinavian American Bank of Fargo, sixty-seven shares, market value $13,400; Peoples State Bank of Grand Forks, eighteen shares, market value $2,160; Peoples State Bank of Casselton, ten shares, market value $1,000; First National Bank of Cheyenne, one hundred twenty-eight shares, market value, $19,200; total, $38,160.[1]

Besides the excessive loans that Halldorson discovered, he found numerous loans that were bad even though not excessive. Space forbids the printing of his comments on this type of loan. Suffice it to say the conclusion was reached that the bank was hopelessly insolvent. As a result of this examination, the State Banking Board ordered the bank closed on October 2 and named Halldorson as temporary receiver. The grounds on which they ordered it closed were first, that the bank was insolvent; and secondly, that it was violating the law in the matter of excessive loans.[2]

Immediately application was made to the Supreme Court by the officers of the bank and the state bank examiner to re-open the bank, and on October 8 the court issued an order pursuant to which State Examiner Lofthus took charge. Lofthus, with the aid of Mr. Myron Thatcher, an accountant, then made an investigation. This examination lasted from October 7 to October 14, 1919. The report of the examination characterized the Halldorson and Sheets report

[1] *House Journal*, 1921, pp. 319, 320.

[2] *Fargo Courier-News*, October 3, 1919.

as incorrect and false in many respects. It reported that a thorough investigation had been made of the bank and that they found its net worth to be $70,000. This was as follows: capital stock, $50,000; surplus, $10,000; accrued profits, $10,000. The report also commented on the loans and arrived at pretty much the opposite conclusions from those contained in Halldorson's report.[1]

On October 22 Lofthus and Thatcher submitted an addendum statement concerning the bank in which the net worth of the bank was shown to be $71,284.71, its reserves as $372,661.91, or $142,500.00 above the legal requirement. Other data was submitted to show an improvement in the bank's condition, and the examiners added as their conclusion that it was in good solvent condition. Upon the basis of this report Lofthus requested that the Court give an order to re-open the bank.[2] The Supreme Court gave the order in an opinion filed on October 24, 1919, and the bank was opened forthwith.

From this opinion two justices dissented. One, Justice Birdzell, "primarily, on the ground of the improper method of conducting the trial; or to speak more accurately, upon the ground that no trial has been had."[3] He held that the defendants had not been permitted by the court to bring to the trial witnesses whose testimony they desired before the court. He believed the whole trial to have been a most extraordinary proceeding in which the defendants had not been given a fair hearing. Whatever the merits of the case might have been, it would seem that the position of the dissenting judges was vindicated when in February, 1921 the Scandinavian American Bank was again closed, this time by officials sympathetic with the League.

[1] *North Dakota Reports*, vol. 46, pp. 470, 471.

[2] *Ibid.*, pp. 472, 473.

[3] *Ibid.*, p. 494.

Enough has been said concerning the Scandinavian American Bank to give the reader an idea of the type of institution that it was, the business it conducted, and its questionable financial strength, at the time when the Bank of North Dakota was so partial to it and favored it above all other banks in the state in the matter of redeposits and loans and rediscounts. The reader can now comprehend the statement of the House Audit Committee made in their report in the following language:

> The general conduct of the bank may best be described as a conduit conveying and carrying the public funds from the Bank of North Dakota in and through the Scandinavian American Bank into the Nonpartisan League and the activities associated with the League.[1]

While this was by all odds the worst example of favoritism in handling the funds of the Bank of North Dakota, it was by no means the only one. There was much testimony given before the House Audit Committee which indicated that the cases of favoritism were numerous.

The fact that so large a sum of redeposits was held in closed banks necessitates comment. The deflation period began in the summer of 1920, and while we have no figures as to the amount of redeposits held by closed banks on the date that this chapter closes, we do have usable figures of a month later. On December 3, 1920 the Bank of North Dakota had a total of \$359,235.63 redeposited in closed banks.[2] This figure swelled rapidly until on February 9, 1921 it had reached \$525,506.52.[3] This appears like a large sum for so early a date in the deflation period. But an ex-

[1] *House Journal* 1921, p. 162.

[2] *Ibid.*, p. 280. On page 238 the amount is given as being substantially \$648,394.

[3] *Ibid.*, p. 280.

amination of the policy of the Bank of North Dakota in placing the redeposits affords a partial explanation.

The examination of a bank in which redeposits were to be placed was not searching. No financial statement was required from the bank. Officers of the Bank of North Dakota would go up to the state bank examiner's office and examine the records there. Or, if it happened that the bank in question had a financial statement on file with the credits department, they might examine that. Little attention was paid to the size of the bank's capital and surplus. The needs of the community and the needs of the bank were considered more weighty than the size of the bank. Even the current condition of the bank seemed of less importance than its past record. For it seems to have been the intention of officers of the Bank of North Dakota to be particularly generous to banks that were hard-pressed by the natural course of business. Take as an example the case of the Beach State Bank. In October, 1920 Mr. O. E. Lofthus, state bank examiner of North Dakota, found the Beach State Bank in a precarious condition. He believed that if it could get $25,000 in cash it might be pulled through its difficulties. So he recommended that that amount be sent to it as a redeposit from the Bank of North Dakota. The redeposit was made and twenty-one days later the bank closed its doors.[1] Among its liabilities were loans and discounts from the Bank of North Dakota to the amount of $20,000, and redeposits from the same source to the sum of $47,735.45.[2]

SUMMARY

In concluding our remarks on the redeposits of the Bank of North Dakota in the first period of its operation we

[1] *House Journal*, 1921, pp. 323, 346.

[2] *Ibid.*, p. 600.

shall again commend the policy of the Bank officials in determining to return public funds to their place of origin and in exceptional cases to favor counties of lesser financial strength. The violation of this policy in the case of Cass county came about because the Bank officials did not formulate and adhere to a wise policy in selecting depositary banks within a county. Their choice of depositary banks must be condemned, for it was influenced by personal and political considerations as typified in the selection of the Scandinavian American Bank of Fargo, and by a desire to rehabilitate the resources of failing banks as typified by the choice of the Beach State Bank and the placing of such large sums in it. In pursuing either policy of choice the Bank officials were violating the first principle of handling a public trust. The funds in question were public funds collected from the citizens for a definite purpose. The custodians of these funds were compelled by law to deposit them in the State Bank. The first and last concern of the Bank should have been to safeguard these public funds in order that they might always be available for withdrawal when desired. These funds should have been redeposited in the strongest, best managed and most conservative banks in the respective counties. Indeed if, because of local circumstances, certain counties did not have banks of first-class strength, such funds should not have been returned to banks in the county at all. Other credit arrangements could have been made for the county in the Bank of North Dakota. It is well-nigh impossible to condemn the Bank's officials too severely for their laxity in examining depositary banks, for their folly in using public funds to succor failing banks, and for the partiality which they showed in the distribution of such funds.

BANK LOANS

The loans that the Bank of North Dakota made during the period under survey may be listed as follows:[1]

1. Farm Loans.
2. Loans to educational and other state institutions pending tax payment.
3. Loans to state and national banks secured by government and state obligations.
4. Rediscounts for depositary banks.
5. Loans to counties for purpose of buying feed and seed for farmers, pending the delivery of county bonds provided for that purpose.
6. Loans to state enterprises, including the Mill and Elevator Association and the Home Builders Association.
7. Loans on warehouse receipts.

GROWTH OF LOANS

The somewhat too condensed statements issued by the Bank make it impossible to trace accurately each of these loans from the beginning. In the case of farm loans it is possible. These grew slowly at first. The reason for this was that few funds were available for this purpose, and the transit department had to be organized first. The bank officials were occupied with this for some months, and it was not until October that farm loans were made in any amount. The September, 1919 statement shows farm loans amounting to $12,497.05, in October $25,472.05, in November $53,669.30, and by the end of the year $127,512.65. In January, 1920 the farm loans jumped to $892,199.04, and thenceforth throughout the year increased steadily and rapidly until the statement for October 15—two weeks before the close of the period here surveyed—the farm loans

[1] *The North Dakota Industrial Program*, The Industrial Commission of North Dakota, June 1, 1920.

totaled $2,905,335.00, and reached their highest level on November 15 at $2,909,788.00.

Unfortunately the 1919 bank statements lumped all the other loans into one under the title "Bills Receivable, Notes and Certificates of Deposit". These grew from $62,581.79 in September, 1919 to $1,151,457.25 in December, 1919. In 1920 these loans are grouped together under the title "Bills Receivable, Rediscounts and Public Transfers", and increase steadily from $1,311,434.21 in January to $2,759,-385.30 in July. Beginning with the August statement these loans are given separately and we have therefore more detailed information about loans at the end of the period studied. The statement for October 15, 1920 shows loans as follows:

Loans to Banks	$2,507,323.90
Loans to Public Institutions and Departments	450,000.00
Loans on Warehouse Receipts	119,277.00
Loans on Real Estate	2,905,335.00

Loans in the strict sense of the term totaled $5,981,935.90

SOURCE OF FUNDS FOR LOANS

All of the loans mentioned in the preceding section were made almost exclusively with the deposits from public corporations and depositary banks. The Bank's capital consisted of the two million dollar bond issue. Provision had been made for issuing mortgage bonds to provide funds for farm loans, and for permanent investment in the state industries and enterprises. But until these could be sold the Bank was forced to make all of its loans from its deposits. A serious miscalculation concerning the salability of these state bonds greatly embarrassed the Bank, for its officials had expected to repay the long-time farm loans, and state industry loans with the proceeds of the bond sales. Thus they would have released the public deposits and bank reserves from long-time investments. A paragraph or two may now be devoted to a statement of the Bank's difficulties in selling the bonds.

THE BANK SELLS REAL ESTATE AND BANK SERIES BONDS

The Bank negotiated a contract for the sale of bonds with Halsey Stuart and Company of Chicago and Wm. R. Compton Co. of St. Louis. This contract called for the delivery of $1,000,000 of real-estate mortgage bonds on January 1, 1920 and like amounts at later dates as soon as they were ready. It also included the sale of the bank series bonds owned for the most part by the Bank itself.[1] The Bank had already sold upwards of $150,000 of bank bonds to parties within the state. The contract with the eastern bond houses, however, required that the entire issue of bank bonds be delivered to them. Accordingly the Bank invited those within the state who had purchased bonds to return them to the Bank for resale with the entire issue. The point was made that by so doing a larger sum of outside money could be brought into the state for use by the Dakotans. As a result of this invitation, nearly $150,000 of bonds were returned and re-purchased by the Bank.[2]

CONSTITUTIONALITY OF NONPARTISAN ACTIVITIES TESTED

However while the bond houses were investigating the legality of the bond issues they contemplated purchasing, certain taxpayers brought suit in the District Court of the United States to enjoin payment of public funds and issuance of bonds by the state. The plaintiffs alleged that their constitutional rights were being infringed upon by such acts. The United States District Court dismissed the bill on its merits, the judge holding that since none of the com-

[1] *Senate Journal*, 1921, p. 793.

[2] *Bank of North Dakota Bulletin*, November, 1919.

plainants alleged individual damages of $3,000 the court had no jurisdiction. Thereupon the case was appealed to the Supreme Court of the United States. The case was argued on April 19 and 20, 1920. On June 1, 1920, the Supreme Court of the United States rendered its decision upholding the decision of the District Court and remanded the case to the District Court with directions to dismiss the bill for want of jurisdiction. Nothing, therefore, was decided or settled by the so-called "Forty-two Taxpayers Suit".[1]

A second suit involving practically all of the issues of the Forty-two Taxpayers Suit was brought in the district court of the state of North Dakota and appealed to the supreme court of the state. This court upheld the constitutionality of the legislation in question at every point. Judge Amidon in rendering the opinion reviewed the economic conditions of North Dakota at considerable length and clearly set forth the reasonableness of the laws whether viewed from an economic or constitutional point of view.

The case was then brought before the Supreme Court of the United States, argued on April 19 and 20, 1920, and decided June 1, 1920. Here again the constitutionality of the legislation in question was fully sustained, the Court holding that,

> If the State sees fit to enter upon such enterprises as are here involved, with the sanction of its constitution, its legislature and its people, we are not prepared to say that it is within the authority of this court in enforcing the observance of the fourteenth amendment to set aside such action by judicial decision.[2]

[1] Scott *vs.* Frasier, *U. S. Reports*, vol. 253.

[2] Green *vs.* Frasier, *ibid.*, vol. 253.

THE BONDS CANNOT BE SOLD

Thus the legality and constitutionality of the bonds were upheld by every court. However, the delay occasioned by the suits was particularly unfortunate, for in the meantime the bond market had greatly weakened and the issues could no longer be sold at the price originally contemplated. Moreover the political situation had become so stormy in North Dakota that there began to be question about safety and adequacy of sinking funds. The result of the whole matter was that the eastern bond houses withdrew their offer and no bonds were sold. This was a serious time for the Bank. The crop failure of 1919 was the worst in several decades. Funds were exceedingly scarce in North Dakota and banks which had rarely ever before asked for rediscounts came to the Bank of North Dakota for loans. Salvation of the whole scheme of the State Bank lay in getting funds into the state. Thwarted in their attempt to sell the bonds, the Bank officials next attempted to negotiate a loan. This they were enabled to do. On July 12, 1920 they borrowed $1,000,000 from the Merchants Loan and Trust Company of Chicago. As security, they hypothecated $1,200,000 of the bank bonds. The loan ran to March 15, 1921 and bore seven per cent interest. Unfavorable as this loan was, it gave the Bank, for the time at least, liquid funds with which it could carry on its banking business, instead of the bonds which it had in reality received as capital.

CRITICISM OF THE BANK LOANS

The loans made by the Bank of North Dakota may be criticized from three points of view. First, were the types of loans proper in view of the types of funds available? Secondly, were the loans granted impartially and without individual favor? Finally, was the security accepted for them proper and sufficient?

A review of the seven types of loans made by the Bank indicates that there were at least two in which the proceeds of the loans were to be invested for a period longer than the Bank of North Dakota was justified in tying up funds raised by taxation for current public needs. Farm loans, and loans to state enterprises should have been made, if at all, on a most restricted scale. The loaning of approximately three and a half millions in long-time investments was unwarranted even though the expectation of sale of real estate and state industry bonds was a reasonable one. The point is that the proceeds of these proposed bond sales were not actually in the Bank's hands and it was contrary to sound banking policy to operate the Bank as if they were.

The short-time loans mentioned above could be properly made with the Bank's deposits, providing of course that they were made in reasonable amounts and were adequately secured.

The other two questions that we have set about to answer —were the loans made impartially and without individual favor, and was the security accepted for them proper and sufficient?—can well be answered together. The answer is that some were and some were not. The farm loans constituted the largest single class of loans. An attempt was made by the attorney for the House Audit Committee to secure testimony that favoritism had been shown in the granting of farm loans.[1] The attempt appears to have been a failure, and there is good reason to believe that farm loans were made impartially and on reasonable security.

But the House Audit Committee found that in the matter of rediscounts the Bank had not pursued so impeccable a course. They discovered rediscounted paper in the Bank that was undesirable from a banking standpoint, and apparently had been accepted by the Bank to favor political

[1] *House Journal*, 1921, pp. 315, 316, 317.

friends. The case of the Michigan City Bank will serve as an example.

When the bank audit was made as of December 3, 1920 there appeared to be six notes, dating from January 18, 1920 to April 13, 1920, and falling due from July 4, 1920 to September 24, 1920, made by the Conway Storage Company of Conway, N. D., to the Michigan City Bank. The face value of the notes totaled $27,800 and the collateral held by the Bank was in the form of storage receipts issued by the Conway Storage Company covering automobiles and tractors in its warehouse.[1] These notes were all long since overdue. The details of their making and how they happened to be in the Bank of North Dakota forms an interesting account which sheds some light on the Bank's loans.

In the village of Conway, one B. H. Stary, operated two businesses. One, under the name of B. H. Stary, was an automobile and tractor agency. The other, under the name of Conway Storage Company, did a bonded-warehouse business. Stary seems to have been on good terms with League leaders, for he boasts of having sold a large number of automobiles to its various leaders and organizers. Early in 1920 he undertook to borrow heavily from the little Michigan City Bank of Michigan City, thirty-eight miles from Conway, and was enabled to do so when he informed the Michigan City Bank officials that he had made arrangements with the Manager of the Bank of North Dakota to rediscount for a local bank the paper they received from Stary, and that loans on warehouse receipts were not limited by law to a certain percentage of the bank's capital and surplus.[2]

[1] The exact value of this security is not certain. Testimony before the House Committee makes it appear that the security was valued at precisely $27,800. But the special Senate Committee claimed that the storage receipts were valued at $31,800. See *House Journal*, 1921, pp. 299-301. Also *Senate Journal*, 1921, p. 779.

[2] *House Journal*, 1921, pp. 541, 552.

Since this paper was overdue the collateral requires comment. It has been said that each note was secured by a storage receipt issued by the Conway Storage Company covering automobiles and tractors in its possession. The Conway Storage Company operated a warehouse bonded by the state for only $5,000. Besides Stary was not particular whether the cars or tractors covered by storage receipts were in the bonded warehouse or in the garage. Moreover he was in the habit of selling automobiles covered by the storage receipts and replacing them in time with other cars that he considered equally valuable. In a word, the fact that the collateral of his notes called for a definite commodity stored in a definite place weighed lightly upon his mind and he paid but little attention to maintaining the letter of the agreement.[1]

The House Audit Committee found a number of other cases similar to the one just described in which paper was rediscounted at the Bank of North Dakota, the funds from which were designed to go to those prominent in the political issues of the state or to league enterprises. But we cannot devote more space to reciting the details of these cases. We must conclude by saying that in the matter of loans and discounts to local banks, the Bank of North Dakota does not have a faultless record of impartiality or of business sagacity.

The House Audit Committee did not reveal any irregularities in the making of loans to individuals on warehouse receipts; and it is therefore safe to conclude that there were none to be found.

The only other loans of importance during the period are listed as "loans to public institutions and departments" and, at the end of the period studied, constituted a total of $450,000 (shortly to be increased to $850,000) loaned to

[1] *House Journal*, 1921, pp. 542, 552, 553, 554, 555, 556.

the Mill and Elevator Association.[1] It will be recalled that the Mill and Elevator Association was permitted to overdraw its account at the Bank and that periodically a note would be given covering the overdraft. This of course was a privilege not accorded to every borrower. The Bank was created to favor these state industries, so it would be improper to criticize the Bank for doing what its founders intended it should do. The notes evidencing these loans were unsecured demand notes made by the Mill and Elevator Association.

A summary of our criticism of the loans of the Bank of North Dakota would lay emphasis on the unwisdom of loaning large sums of demand deposits of public funds on longtime investments, even if there was an expectation of funds from bond sales to take up the loans. It would call attention to the fact that the Bank of North Dakota was led into making numerous loans to banks, which cannot be explained except in a way which indicates that they were partially made to political friends, in amounts and upon terms that could not be defended as being wise or prudent. In short, the Bank's policy to help the hard-pressed farmers and to establish new financial and industrial machinery was not tempered by mature reflective prudence. The enthusiasm of the new order ran away with men's better judgment and led them to loan the public funds without due consideration of when or how they could be repaid. The result was that when the audit was made as of December 3, 1920, the total of past due loans was $1,405,438.32; and while $12,854.86 had been collected in the form of interest and one per cent amortization payments, yet a larger sum, $16,764.00, was past due on the same account.[2]

[1] *House Journal*, 1921 pp. 292, 293.

[2] *Ibid.*, p. 282.

RESERVES

The Bank Act contains no dictum relating to reserves. Neither was the Bank obliged to conform to the law applicable to the state banks. The Bank officials were free to pursue their own policy regarding the amount and type of reserve against liabilities that they would maintain. It is interesting to note the proportion of cash to the demand and time liabilities that was kept in the absence of any legal requirements; and we may take the liberal reserve law applicable to the state banks of North Dakota as a guide in our attempt to estimate the reasonableness of the Bank's reserves. An abbreviated section of the law follows:

Each corporation or association shall at all times have on hand in available funds an amount which shall equal 10 per cent of its demand deposits and amounts due to other banks and 7 per cent of its time deposits; three-fifths of this amount may consist of balances due to the corporation or association from the Bank of North Dakota, or good solvent state or national banks or trust companies, which carry sufficient reserve to entitle them to act as such depositary banks, and are located in such commercial centers as will facilitate the purposes of banking exchanges, . . . and the remaining two-fifths of such reserve shall consist of actual cash on hand; cash items shall not be included in computing reserve, and no corporation or association shall carry as cash or cash items, any paper or other matter except legitimate bank exchange, which will be cleared on the same or next succeeding day. . . . [1]

The published bank statements of the first year's operations are too condensed to permit us to procure the necessary data. Therefore we will confine our inquiries to four months beginning with August, 1920. This we believe to be a fair sample, and will give us results that are representative of the Bank's condition during the entire period. The following figures are important.

[1] *Special Session Laws of 1919*, chap. 23.

	August	September	October	November
Due to depositary banks (reserves)	$1,719,067.62	$1,664,399.47	$2,005,374.32	$1,392,498.68
Public deposits (general)	12,025,637.53	11,078,291.20	10,752,287.60	11,559,039.01
Public deposits (sinking funds)..	3,333,285.93	3,408,829.85	3,400,855.40	3,365,548.66
Individual deposits............	97,927.68	111,056.89	189,027.35	214,926.33
Cash on hand and cash items...	53,173.87	42,217.26	55,380.99	57,433.09
Due from depositary banks in North Dakota (redeposits)...	10,605,782.21	9,148,100.26	8,871,436.72	8,407,484.63
Due from correspondent banks outside North Dakota	526,135.46	432,888.73	586,616.14	580,602.14
Collection items due from banks in the state	1,071,661.93	1,351,622.75	1,652,809.78	2,253,882.29
Collection items due from the state and public corporations..	29,619.93	97,889.60	76,692.00	74,333.92

The deposits may now be grouped together according to whether they represent demand or time deposits. Thus added together the items "due to depositary banks (reserves)" and "Public deposits, general and other funds" we get the total for demand deposits. Similarly adding together the items "public deposits (sinking funds)" and "individual deposits" (mainly time deposits) we get the total for time deposits. These results may then be tabulated for the four months as follows:

	August	September	October	November
Demand deposits	$13,744,705.15	$12,742,690.67	$12,757,661.92	$12,951,537.69
Time deposits	3,431,213.61	3,519,886.74	3,589,882.75	3,580,474.99
Total	$17,175,918.76	$16,261,577.41	$16,347,544.67	$16,532,012.68

When percentages are struck it appears that the cash on hand and cash items amount to an average of only three-tenths of one per cent of the total deposits, of which about eighty per cent were demand deposits.

Let us now compute the reserves necessary to satisfy the law that an ordinary state bank in North Dakota would be obliged to maintain if it held similar deposits.

	August	September	October	November
Ten per cent of its demand deposits would be.............	$1,374,470.52	$1,274,269.07	$1,275,766.19	$1,295,153.77
Seven per cent of its time deposits would be.............	240,184.95	246,392.07	251,291.79	250,633.25
Total reserve required ...	$1,614,655.47	$1,520,661.14	$1,527,057.98	$1,545,787.02
Of this not less than two-fifths must be in cash in the bank or	645,862.19	608,264.45	610,823.19	618,214.81
Three-fifths in other designated banks	968,793.28	912,396.67	916,234.79	927,372.21

It will be seen at once that if the North Dakota law on bank reserves had been applied to the Bank of North Dakota it would have been considerably short of the required cash, and when it is recalled that the law permits other funds to be counted as reserve only when lodged in "the Bank of North Dakota, or good solvent state or national banks or trust companies which carry sufficient reserve to entitle them to act as such depositary banks, and are located in such commercial centers as will facilitate the purposes of banking exchanges," then it appears that, because of the universal lack of reserves on the part of North Dakota depositary banks, and their rural position, the reserve of the Bank of North Dakota was only a fraction of the legal requirement for other state banks.

The conclusion is that in the absence of legal requirements the reserves of the Bank of North Dakota were allowed to shrink far more than sound banking practice warranted. State and national banks are required by law to keep on hand at all times, in cash and in approved depositaries, certain percentages of their demand and time deposits. Federal reserve banks are required to keep as much as thirty-five per cent of their deposits in cash in their own vaults. This is a wholesome and necessary protection safeguarding the interests of depositors. The enormity of the error of leaving such a provision out of the North Dakota Bank Act was amply demonstrated when the cash holdings of the Bank and its deposits in strong, well-located banks were allowed to dwindle almost to the vanishing point. The absence of a law requiring a reasonable reserve was without doubt largely responsible for many of the difficulties that the Bank encountered.

EARNINGS OF THE BANK

The income of the Bank was almost exclusively derived from the spread of the interest paid on deposits and that charged by the Bank on loans and redeposits. Practically none was derived from exchange or other sources.[1] The following table gives the interest rates paid by the Bank on various deposits as well as those charged by the Bank on its various loans and redeposits.

INTEREST RATES—EFFECTIVE JULY 1, 1919[2]

To be paid by The Bank of North Dakota:

1. On daily balances subject to check (from outside the State of North Dakota) averaging $300 per month or more	2%
2. On daily balances subject to check (banks and public corporations), crediting items on date of receipt and charging costs of collection, if any	2%
3. On daily balances subject to check (banks and public corporations within the state), deferring credit until items are collected and charging costs of collection, if any	2¼%
4. On time deposits (sinking funds), public corporations	4%
5. On time certificates of deposit (from outside the State of North Dakota), amounting to $500 or more, deposited for six months or one year	4%

[1] *House Journal*, 1921, p. 234.

[2] *The Bank of North Dakota*, p. 45. This is Rule 4.

To be charged by The Bank of North Dakota:

6. On daily balances in Depositary Banks	4%
7. On time certificates of deposit (from Depositary Banks) secured by collateral	6%
8. On re-discounts from Depositary Banks, or on money borrowed secured by collateral other than State or Government obligations, not exceeding six months	6%
9. On money borrowed (by Depositary Banks) secured by State or Government obligations, not exceeding three months	5%
10. On farm loans (7% installment to be paid annually)	6%

There has been a good deal of controversy about the Bank's earnings, and much has been said and written to prove both that the Bank has and has not shown a profit. While the original Bank officials were in power they constantly and stoutly maintained that the Bank was more than paying its way, while it was furnishing credit to the farmers at rates of interest theretofore unknown in North Dakota. Typical of this view is the excerpt from an article in the Bank's bulletin for August, 1920.

If regarded purely as a business proposition The Bank of North Dakota has achieved a success during its first year that would have been regarded as phenomenal if it had been a private bank. The total net earnings of the Bank at the close of business on August 14th (representing approximately one year's business) amounted to $241,838.41.
These earnings are distributed as follows:

Conveyed to surplus	$40,000.00
Reserve to pay amount of legislative appropriation used by the Bank	23,954.10
Reserve for depreciation on furniture and fixtures	6,467.99
Reserve to pay interest due Jan. 1st and July 1st, 1921 on $2,000,000 of Bank series bonds	100,000.00
Undivided profits	71,416.32

Computed on its capital stock the net earnings of The Bank of North Dakota amount to more than 12 per cent annually.

But such statements were by no means accepted as conclusive by those who were less sympathetic towards the Bank. The *Fargo Forum* commented on the Bank's earnings as follows:

The bank has actually lost hundreds of thousands of dollars. It claims to show a paper profit of some $200,000, but this is based on the theory that every transaction it has made will be 100 per cent sound. Nothing is charged off for losses in bankrupt banks; nothing has been charged off for losses on real estate loans. And even if the so-called "profits" were admitted, they are nothing but an indirect tax on the people of the state, for which no service has been returned by the bank.[1]

The difference in conclusions reached by these opposing writers is evidently the result of a difference in conception of the value of the item "interest earned and not collected", and as to the propriety of considering all the paper assets of the Bank as actually existing intact when it was well known that many Bank funds were tied up in insolvent banks. No one can deny that a conservative statement would make allowance for the possibility of loss on such items. At all events the most that could be said is that such profits as were indicated by the Bank were paper profits. Subsequent events proved the correctness of those who maintained that the Bank was not making an actual profit. The lack of actual profit is, however, not necessarily a reflection on the Bank's management. A public institution might well be run at a loss and still be run efficiently. The Bank officials, however, intended the Bank to show a profit. The reasons that it did not actually do so are to be found in the losses that the Bank sustained through unwise loans and redeposits, factors which took on added importance as deflation swept the state.

[1] *Mountain States Banker*, April 1921, p. 34, reprint of an editorial in the *Fargo Forum*.

CHAPTER VI

Operation of the Bank of North Dakota from November 2, 1920 to November 2, 1921

GENERAL CONSIDERATIONS

To understand the events of these twelve months it is necessary to bear in mind that while the Bank was apparently prospering during the entire period from its beginning to the time when the Public Fund Law was passed, it nevertheless was pursuing a banking policy which was rapidly bringing it into a very critical condition;—a position, indeed, which might not terminate in disaster if nothing arose to test its strength, but one which was sure to cause trouble in case anything out of the ordinary came to pass. The Bank had permitted a far too large proportion of its funds to be tied up in long-time investments and in redeposits with which the local banks were equally prodigal. The Bank's assets were far from liquid.

Moreover, it must be borne in mind that outside forces were already at work undermining the Bank's foundations, which at best were none too secure to bear the inflated institution. Politicians opposed to the Nonpartisan League, and what it stood for, had begun a relentless campaign against the Bank, and had spread unlimited propaganda designed to curtail the Bank's operations and success. Then deflation overtook the state. Thus the enemies of the Bank suddenly found themselves possessed of a powerful ally with whose involuntary aid they could shortly push the institution to the very brink of destruction.

It is unnecessary to enlarge upon the reasons why deflation came just when it did. But a paragraph or two devoted to describing the significance of the political attack on the Bank will not be amiss. For, in a way, it seems almost incredible that a State Bank should draw so much fire from a political faction. Yet it must be borne in mind that deflation rapidly and ruthlessly placed the farmers in a serious financial condition, and forced the local banks into a no less miserable situation. Now, if responsibility for this condition could be attached to the Bank of North Dakota and the losses of the farmers be laid at its door, there would be no question that those who were responsible for its operation would speedily be voted out of office and their opponents voted in. Nothing oppressed the voters of North Dakota during this period as much as the relentless progress of deflation. The political opponents of the State Administration saw their chance to use this unexpected misfortune to their political advantage.

DEFLATION BEGINS

The gradual recession of prices which had begun in May, 1920 in certain wholesale commodities became evident in the farm products which North Dakota marketed by the middle of July. Throughout the harvesting and threshing season the prices of grain continued steadily downward. Local bankers and Bank of North Dakota officials urged the farmers to hold their grain for better prices. This advice commended itself to the farmers, and accordingly the so-called sellers' strike began. Few believed that the price of grain would not improve because the cost of producing the crop had been high. Current grain prices would not equal the cost of production. Moreover, late summer weather conditions were bad, so that the bright prospects for a better-than-normal crop were shattered. There would not be a bumper crop to depress the market.

NORTH DAKOTA BANKS COLLAPSE UNDER STRAIN

However, as the season wore away, prospects for better prices were not encouraging. The car shortage, which had been acute all summer, was now holding up the movement of the new crop. Credit conditions were extremely stringent. The price of grain steadily fell. Farmers could not sell except with great loss and the obligations at the local banks were not being met. The credit extended by the local banks was being frozen in a rapidly depreciating commodity, and one bank after the other was compelled to close its doors.

THE INITIATED PUBLIC FUND LAW

With the financial situation of the state in this strained and precarious condition, a law was initiated on November 2, 1920 which multiplied the difficulties of the Bank of North Dakota and through it the strain on many local banks.

The opponents of the Bank of North Dakota had, by the November elections, succeeded in enlisting a sufficient number of electors in their cause to initiate a law which in effect made any and all state and national banks in North Dakota legal depositaries of the public funds of the various counties, townships, school districts, cities and villages. The Bank of North Dakota was thereby forced to compete on a par with the local banks for the deposits of the public funds of the political subdivisions of the state. This was a tremendous blow to the Bank because it opened the way for the removal of its largest and most reliable deposits. All now depended on whether or not the treasurers of the local political subdivisions were friendly or hostile to the Bank.

But, while this law might easily prove to be very embarrassing to the Bank, it also contained dangerous possibilities for the local banks. If public funds were withdrawn in large amounts from the Bank, it in turn would be forced to withdraw from the local banks the funds it had redeposited in them. This added to the heavy credit strain under which the local banks were already laboring would have proved to have been the last straw in a great number of cases. The banking situation in North Dakota was serious indeed.

COMMON PERIL BEGETS COOPERATION

The consequence was that the winter of 1920-21 witnessed a common peril driving together factions that theretofore had been at swords' points; and a reasonable amount of cooperation appeared to be forthcoming. The Public Fund Law had scarcely taken effect when the bankers throughout the state met at Bismarck and Fargo and advised and urged county and city treasurers to allow their deposits to remain with the Bank of North Dakota, and to withdraw only such funds as were absolutely necessary for current needs. Nonpartisan League members and members of the opposition were entreated to forget politics for the time being and to cooperate in warding off impending financial ruin. United action was urged to save the state.[1]

BANKERS' CONFERENCES AND PROPOSALS

Several conferences between the Bank officials and the local bankers followed. Thus, early in December, they met in Bismarck and proposals for a Bankers Finance Corporation to market state securities were roughly outlined.[2] About this same time the local bankers held their convention in Bismarck. The North Dakota Bankers Association which theretofore had held itself hostile to and aloof from the State Bank's affairs now adopted a resolution pledging its aid in the sale of the various bond issues which were

[1] *Wall Street Journal*, December 6, 1920, and January 6, 1921; *The Financier*, December 1, 1920.

[2] *Commercial West*, December 25, 1920.

still in the hands of the Bank of North Dakota. On December 14 a committee was appointed to investigate the market in the East and elsewhere, to determine whether or not, and upon what conditions, the various state, county and minor political subdivisions' securities could be sold. The State Administration asked particularly that an effort be made to sell $3,000,000 of Farm Mortgage bonds, $2,000,000 Bank of North Dakota bonds, $2,000,000 Mill and Elevator Association bonds, and $250,000 Home Builders Association bonds. After nearly a month's investigation of market conditions, the Bankers Committee on January 7 submitted the following report and proposal to the Industrial Commission and Bank of North Dakota:

To the Honorable Industrial Commission and The Bank of North Dakota:

The committee of bankers invited under date of December 30, last, to confer with you with the view of devising some means of selling available securities and bettering the financial situation thruout the state, beg to submit the following:

Thru the numerous conferences of the past month it would appear that the most immediate and important question is the sale of the several issues of the state bonds now being offered.

The bankers have earnestly endeavored to assist in the sale of these bonds but so far without success; the administration has also been unable to sell them. The bankers have ascertained the conditions under which these bonds could now be sold by them and with these conditions before them make the proposition:

The bankers will undertake to sell $3,000,000 of farm loan bonds as well as the balance of the $10,000,000 as reasonably needed and the market will absorb.

Two million dollars of the mill and elevator bonds to complete and put into operation the Grand Forks mill and elevator.

Two hundred and fifty thousand dollars of home building bonds.

One million dollars of the Bank of North Dakota bonds.

To bring this about on the part of the administration it will be necessary:

To limit the operation of the Bank of North Dakota to the administration of state, state institutions, and state industry finances; farm loan and farm loan bonds.

To procure the enactment of a new depository law for counties, townships, school districts, boards of education, villages and cities, making every going bank a permanent public depository and fixing the rate of interest by statute, providing also for publicity as an assurance that the deposits would be properly distributed.

To provide some assurance to the public that the so-called farmers' industrial program will be confined to the Grand Forks mill and elevator, to the Drake mill and to the Bank of North Dakota, and that no state indebtedness other than the above be created during the term of the present administration.

To confer with attorneys for bond buyers at an early date and if any new or amendatory legislation, or order of the Industrial Commission, is required to make the bonds more readily marketable, to see that it is provided.[1]

The committee made the following comments in their report to the North Dakota Bankers Association, by way of explanation of their proposal to the Industrial Commission:

a. [The] farm loan bonds your committee found readily saleable. These were not looked upon as a direct indebtedness of the state, and the contingent liability only very slight. The entire $10,000,000 authorized by the constitution can be readily sold and should be sold and their sale would not damage the states credit. Your committee proposes to sell all of them subject only to the conditions hereafter set forth:

b. Your committee found [the Grand Forks mill and elevator] bonds to be very difficult of sale, but had proffers for this amount ($2,000,000) if the so-called industrial program could be limited until a fair trial should determine whether or

[1] *Bank of North Dakota Bulletin*, January, 1921.

not the mill and elevator business under state ownership would be profitable.

c. Homebuilding bonds . . . were considered in the same case as the farm loan bonds.

d. Your committee was unable to find a market for any [Bank of North Dakota Bonds] but took it for granted that if an agreement could be reached, in order to bring it about, the banks of the state would if necessary attempt to dispose of . . . $1,000,000 [of them].[1]

Finally the Bankers Committee explained to the Industrial Commission and Bank officials the conditions under which the bankers of North Dakota would undertake the sale of the above-mentioned bonds. They pointed out that,

Prospective buyers were unanimous in insisting that the laws under which the Bank of North Dakota was organized and as now construed by the Industrial Commission were unwise, not conducive to sound banking and unless materially amended would at all times be a menace to the financial system of the state, and would frequently bring about just such conditions as now exist. That no proper safeguards were thrown about the trust funds. That under the law such funds could and would be, as they have now been, transferred, loaned or invested in enterprises where they would not be available when required. All safeguards by previous laws thrown around sinking funds had been removed, and no adequate substitute provided.[2]

THE INDUSTRIAL COMMISSION'S REPLY

To these objections the Industrial Commission took exception, denied their validity, and urged that there was no ground for criticism of the administration of public funds. The following reply to the Bankers' Committee shows their attitude toward these proposals.[3]

[1] *Fargo Forum*, January 19, 1921.

[2] *Ibid.*

[3] *Bank of North Dakota Bulletin*, January, 1921.

We wish to assure the committee that we appreciate the interest it has taken in this matter. The proposition, however, cannot honorably be considered by the commission for the reason that it is a plain attempt on the part of financial interests, presumably Wall Street financiers, to dictate the political, financial and industrial policies of the State of North Dakota, and requiring a surrender of the sovereign powers of the state to manage its own affairs, and to permit the dictation and interference with the independence and liberty of the free people of a sovereign state.

The time has not yet arrived when any group, no matter how powerful financially, can dictate to this state how to manage its own affairs. Every state in the United States is guaranteed a republican form of government under our constitution. The officers of the state, even though elected by the people, have no authority to surrender its sovereignty. Rights once surrendered are seldom if ever regained.

We are satisfied that any group of men that would exact such a surrender and arrogate to themselves the prerogative of making the laws for the people of the state would rule with a tyrannical hand.

The bonds of North Dakota can, and will, be sold without a surrender or compromise of this nature. We are satisfied that your committee did not expect the industrial commission to accept the terms and conditions in the above communication, as some of your members frankly admitted. We are positive that in the near future, with your cooperation, these bonds will sell readily. There is no better security anywhere in the United States. Many men of influence and wealth outside of the state are seriously considering the purchase of these bonds just as soon as the present financial stringency passes.

Yours very sincerely,

THE INDUSTRIAL COMMISSION,

Lynn J. Frazier,
John N. Hagan,
William Lemke.

Thus the cooperation of local bankers and state officials came to an unfortunate end.

THE EFFECTS OF THE PUBLIC FUND LAW

Shortly after the initiated law made possible the depositing of public funds of minor political subdivisions in banks other than the Bank of North Dakota, a resolution was adopted by the Industrial Commission which interpreted the Public Fund Law as being not retroactive.[1] In other words, it was held that money already on deposit in the Bank of North Dakota could not be withdrawn for the purpose of depositing it elsewhere. Acting under authority of this resolution, the officials of the Bank refused to honor drafts drawn by public treasurers of the minor political subdivisions, when they were obviously drawn for the purpose of removing the funds to local banks.[2] Thus the effort immediately to withdraw county and other political subdivision money was effectually blocked. The result was that the public deposits did not fall disastrously at once, but embarrassment would arise from the lack of future deposits of public funds. The statements of the Bank show the wasting away of these deposits. The November 15 statement shows a total deposit of all public funds, exclusive of sinking funds, amounting to $11,559,039.01. On December 15 the total public deposits amounted to $9,523,630. The inference is that the greater part of this loss was in the accounts of the minor political subdivisions. After December, 1920 the figures are given separately for the state and for the minor political subdivisions. The following table shows the manner in which the deposits of the latter fell away.[3]

[1] *House Journal*, 1921, p. 192.

[2] *New York Times*, December 7, 1920, January 3, 1921.

[3] Figures taken from monthly bank statements in *Bank of North Dakota Bulletins*.

January 15	$4,840,896.33
February 16	3,821,835.15
March 16	3,687,648.42
April 15	2,860,129.54
May 16	2,266,417.97
June 16	1,758,294.02
July 16	1,543,403.01
August 16	1,253,711.02
September 16	1,064,902.81
October 15	1,420,100.35
November 15	1,932,298.54
November 23	1,902,605.91

The difficulty in stemming this ebb of deposits was that it was not so easy to devise a way to prevent the removal of public funds when the draft drawn by a public treasurer was in payment for some current expenditure. However, on December 20, 1920, the Industrial Commission adopted a resolution "that the Bank of North Dakota be and is hereby instructed until further order from this commission to discontinue honoring checks drawn by such county and other treasurers who have discontinued making their deposits with the Bank of North Dakota."[1] This action was taken in order to block a practice, already begun by treasurers, of depositing the new tax money in local banks while continuing to check out funds from the Bank of North Dakota for current needs. The Industrial Commission justified its action because of "the emergency . . . created"[2] by the non-cooperation of many of the treasurers. So the Bank of North Dakota would write "illegally drawn" across the face of such treasurer's checks and return them unhonored.[3]

Moreover, in some cases in which the treasurer was not hostile, a way was devised for economizing funds. The failure of the state treasurer to call the hail warrants is a

[1] *House Journal*, 1921, p. 192.

[2] *Ibid.*, p. 192.

[3] *Ibid.*, p. 236.

case in point. Under the North Dakota State Hail Insurance Law, claims are made to the state auditor who issues warrants on the funds held by the state treasurer. These then are registered in the order of their presentation and subsequently paid in the same order. They bear six per cent interest until paid.

When the Public Fund Law of November 2, 1920 took away the monopoly of public deposits from the Bank of North Dakota, there remained still unpaid of the 1919 hail loss claims roughly $1,000,000. At the same time the hail fund amounted to about $145,000. This grew rapidly. By November 30 it amounted to $437,905.12, by December 30 to $772,828.08, and a month later to upwards of $788,000. Meanwhile after October 30 the state treasurer called no warrants for payment.[1] Since the funds were kept on deposit in the Bank of North Dakota this delay in calling the hail warrants was of great benefit to the Bank.[2]

But in spite of all efforts to the contrary, the deposits of the treasurers of the political subdivisions fell away. In the month between January 15 and February 16 these deposits fell more than one million dollars, or nearly twenty-seven per cent. This dwindling of deposits was alarming enough to cause a second conference of private bankers with representatives of the Bank of North Dakota. On February 13, 1921 representatives of the Bank met with private bankers of North Dakota and representatives of Minneapolis financial institutions. At this conference the problem of the sale of the state bonds again surpassed all others in importance. The private bankers were reluctant to accept responsibility for their sale, demurring on the

[1] *Bank of North Dakota Bulletin*, January, 1920; *Commercial West*, January 22, 1921.

[2] *The Fargo Courier-News*, January 9, 1921 reports $750,000 in the Hail Insurance Fund on deposit in the Bank of North Dakota, and $1,110,085.63 due to farmers from unpaid 1919 hail warrants.

grounds that there probably was doubt as to the validity of the issues, and because they feared that the public would be unwilling purchasers of these bonds. Three reasons were advanced for this belief. First, the bonds had already been "hawked about" in the Chicago and New York markets by irresponsible individuals; secondly, the present government of North Dakota did not meet with the approval of investors; finally, the intense bitterness of the political struggle in North Dakota had injured the public's faith in the bonds.

However, the Minneapolis bankers were not without a plan. They proposed to find a market for state bonds to the amount of $6,000,000 on condition that the following general policy be put into effect.[1]

1. The Nonpartisan leaders were to enact laws that would permit the liquidation of the Bank of North Dakota to a farm-loan institution only.
2. They were to pass laws that would make the sale of state bonds possible. (No doubt reference was here made to laws protecting sinking funds, etc.)
3. They were to pass laws which would safeguard public moneys in private banks and make the Bank of North Dakota ineligible to receive public money.
4. The North Dakota Home Builders Association was to be dissolved immediately upon the completion of the work under construction.
5. The Industrial Program was to be restricted to the building and operation of the flour mill and elevator at Grand Forks.

[1] *Commercial West*, February 19, 1921; *New York Times*, February 16-17, 1921; *The Nation*, March 9, 1921; *New Republic*, March 9, 1921; *Fargo Courier-News*, February 15, 1921. The *Fargo Courier-News* reported that Minneapolis "bankers would undertake to sell $2,000,000 bank series bonds . . . and to provide a $1,000,000 fund for financing the operation of the state mill and elevator . . . seek a market for $2,500,000 of mill and elevator bonds and back the sale of $3.000,000 farm loan bonds."

The representatives of the Bank and of the State Administration were tempted to agree to this proposal and thus reach a compromise. But they rightly pointed out that the only body that had authority to change existing laws was the state legislature itself. Furthermore, they argued that if funds could be obtained by the sale of bonds so that the state industries could be financed without the State Bank's aid, then, automatically, the Bank of North Dakota would become virtually only a farm-loan bank. These arguments, however, were not convincing to the Minneapolis and North Dakota private bankers and the conference ended without definite results.

Meanwhile the financial situation in North Dakota was becoming worse and worse. The situation was admittedly so serious that the entire March Bank Bulletin, aside from the usual bank statement, was given over to an article entitled, "Our Financial Dilemma and the Way Out". In this article the management of the Bank admitted that the situation was intolerable, and briefly analyzed it as follows:

1. That in many localities in the state farmers have not had a full crop for three or four years, and in some localities losses have been practically total for three or four years;

2. That, owing to the disastrous slump in farm prices, many of the farmers in these localities are unable to pay their obligations in full, even by selling the whole of this year's crop;

3. That even in districts where the 1920 crop was normal, reductions in prices have very seriously impaired the ability of farmers to meet their obligations;

4. That in order to avoid selling below cost, many farmers are holding their grain for better prices and thus delaying liquidation of credit;

5. That, owing to disturbed conditions in the state and the dissemination of confused and contradictory, if not false, statements outside of the state, investors have hesitated to send their money to North Dakota;

6. That the carrying out of the will of the people as expressed in the Bank Act, passed by the 1919 session of the legislature and approved by the people on referendum, has resulted in the redistribution of public deposits in banks, and in the temporary tying up of a portion of the funds of the Bank of North Dakota in long-time loans to farmers and loans to state industries;

7. That the carrying out of this policy necessitated cooperation on the part of public corporations, as well as of banks, and that that cooperation has not, in most instances, been forthcoming;

8. That the adoption of the initiated law, making optional the depositing of county and local public funds in the Bank, and providing no depositary banks to which the funds could be removed, has very seriously embarrassed The Bank of North Dakota and has added greatly to the difficulties of local banks;

9. That instead of bringing forward a constructive plan, or in good faith supporting the plan adopted by The Bank of North Dakota and approved by the Bankers' Convention in December for the relief of the situation, the opposition to the Bank has carried on a relentless campaign of unfair criticism, of ruthless exposures of confidential relations, under the pretense of a necessary investigation, and of misleading propaganda, in and out of the state, with regard to the acts and purposes of the state administration and The Bank of North Dakota;

10. That the opposition has laid down conditions for its cooperation with the Administration which mean nothing less than the destruction of the Bank and the emasculation of the Industrial Program, thus rendering acceptance by the Administration impossible, since by such acceptance they would prove false to the trust the people have reposed in them;

11. That there are many banks in the state which are unable to meet their obligations, and that, as a result, the Bank of North Dakota is able only in part to meet the drafts of public corporations;

12. That the actions of certain public treasurers in garnisheeing funds of the Bank of North Dakota in local banks serves only to further increase the difficulties of those banks and their patrons, and to delay the orderly liquidation of county and local funds;

13. That bonds of the state, provided for financing state industries and enterprises and for the making of real estate loans must be sold before funds can be replaced in the Bank of North Dakota, and work on the state industries resumed.

BANK BEGINS TO REGISTER CHECKS

The million-dollar note, which the Merchants Loan and Trust Company of Chicago held because of the loan made to the Bank of North Dakota on July 12, 1920, fell due on March 15, 1921 and was paid. As early as February 10 the Industrial Commission had issued an order to the Bank of North Dakota commanding it to force collection of funds in local banks, and register all state treasurer's checks excepting those in payment for the ordinary expenses of state penal, charitable and educational institutions.[1] Now, in order to meet the Chicago note, it was necessary for the Bank "to restrict the payment of [political subdivision] treasurer's checks and warrants, where treasurers were discounting their accounts, to the payment of ordinary expenses of state and local educational and charitable institutions and for the payment of installments and interest of bonds and warrants and other necessary purposes."[2] Meanwhile the other checks of treasurers were registered for future payment, and bore six per cent interest from the date of presentation until paid. This was "admittedly a drastic policy to meet a temporary situation."[3] But the Bank offi-

[1] *Fargo Courier-News*, February 11, 1921.

[2] *Bank of North Dakota Bulletin*, March, 1921.

[3] *Ibid.*, June, 1921.

cials justified it in several ways. It was the only means of averting a great financial catastrophe and, therefore, justifiable. There was a precedent for the policy in that the big New York banks had, in 1907, under similarly acute circumstances, refused to pay checks over their counters and had not even paid interest on such deposits during the interim. The result was then, as it appeared now, that only by this method could serious financial calamity be averted. Furthermore there was a fundamental difference between private banks and a state-owned bank which justified the registering of checks.

> The transactions of the former are based on pre-existing revenues. . . . A bank owned and operated by the State is analogous to any other political subdivision of the State, or to the State itself, whose business transactions are frequently based on anticipated revenues. . . . If the State itself may register warrants for future payment, the State operating through the Bank of North Dakota may with equal propriety do the same thing, when it is necessary for the protection of the financial interests of the State and its people.[1]

Finally, when the critical condition within the state might have been relieved through delaying the payment of the obligation in Chicago, it was thought better to maintain the credit of the state abroad even at the expense of greater embarrassment at home.

The registered checks first appeared in the bank statement of the Bulletin for April. Succeeding statements show that they varied in amounts as follows:[2]

[1] *Bank of North Dakota Bulletin*, June, 1921.

[2] Figures taken from the monthly bank statements in the *Bank of North Dakota Bulletins*.

April, 1921	$139,705.18
May	93,770.90
June	72,873.44
July	215,510.90
August	209,706.89
September	179,692.84
October	34,227.27
November 16	11,960.56
November 23	10,885.65

On September 27 the Bank announced that it was ready to pay all registered checks, and that the payment of interest on them would cease October 7. Its ability to pay these checks was attributed to "increased individual deposits, to a substantial liquidation of so-called 'frozen' loans and redeposits in banks, and to continued progress in bond sales." A small amount of them continued to appear in subsequent statements because they were not presented for payment. The Bank was prepared to meet them.

THE BANK'S STRUGGLE FOR SOLVENCY

When the Minneapolis Bankers' Conference ended without satisfactory plans for the Bank's relief, the state and Bank officials gave up all hope of getting private bankers either in North Dakota or elsewhere to cooperate with them without making too great concessions. They determined to abandon all financial machinery that might exist in the country and fight their way back to solvency and liquidity alone. This could be attempted in three ways. In the first place they could endeavor to force the local banks to pay up the overdue loans and redeposits which at this time amounted to about three million dollars. Secondly, they could attempt to increase deposits greatly. Finally, they could attempt to sell the state bonds.

The political storm that had been beating against the Bank of North Dakota from the beginning, damaging its reputation and credit, grew in fury as month succeeded month.

The Public Fund Law of November 2, 1920, imperilled the very foundation of the Bank, for it was the public deposits upon which the Bank was relying and upon which its credit structure was, in the main, built. Moreover at this same election an initiated law was passed providing for an audit of the Bank of North Dakota and the other state industries. Three months later the House Audit Committee began the investigation of the Bank's condition and management. The members of the State Administration knew well that any unhealthy condition of the Bank would be revealed and would be used against them politically. The financial woes that had overtaken the state would, rightly or wrongly, be saddled upon them. Small wonder then, that on February 10 the Industrial Commission should have issued an order to the Bank of North Dakota commanding it to force collection of the funds that it had either redeposited in, or loaned to the local banks.[1] For, if it proved that the local banks could not pay their demand obligations to the State Bank, a large part of the blame for the financial crisis could be shifted on to the shoulders of the local bankers. So the local banks were subjected to pressure in an attempt either to recover the funds loaned to, and redeposited in them, or to embarrass and establish the blame upon them. The table printed below shows that by mid-summer the local banks had given up practically all that they could possibly pay.

The Bank went on record in July as opposing any further drastic pressure on the depositary banks for the reason that such pressure would ruin them and make the financial crisis no less severe. At the same time the Bank served notice on the local banks that this lenient policy would last only until after harvest, when the farmers would be able to pay them, and they, in turn, could pay the Bank of North Dakota.[2] As

[1] *Fargo Courier-News*, February 11, 1921.

[2] *Ibid.*, July 19, 1921.

a matter of fact the Bank never again resorted to drastic measures, for after harvest substantial aid had come from another direction. The following table shows Bank of North Dakota redeposits within the state for the year 1921 up to the time when the Nonpartisan officials gave way to the Independents.[1]

	Redeposits				*Loans*
January 15	$6,204,526.67	in	793	banks	$2,607,418.03
February 16	4,939,045.43	"	785	"	2,464,041.38
March 16	4,038,439.75	"	641	"	2,312,865.05
April 15	3,474,959.29	"	573	"	2,222,856.22
May 16	2,991,351.60	"	470	"	2,161,589.27
June 16	2,787,705.54	"	374	"	2,059,071.41
July 16	2,511,491.74	"	290	"	2,016,871.32
August 16	2,406,137.99	"	272	"	2,020,913.88
September 16	2,243,280.70	"	214	"	1,919,397.56
October 15	2,200,844.43	"	208	"	1,862,168.43
November 15	2,211,993.38	"	211	"	1,809,172.73
November 23	2,118,244.82	"	208	"	1,902,513.50

DRIVE FOR INDIVIDUAL DEPOSITS

The drive for individual deposits was begun in the latter part of February, 1921. Up to this time it had been the avowed policy of the Bank of North Dakota not to receive individual deposits from residents of North Dakota. Such deposits " should be made in the established other financial institutions ".[2] Furthermore, it was contrary to the Bank's policy to establish branches. " The voluntary opening of accounts by state and national banks with the Bank of North Dakota [would] establish a branch or depository relationship." [3] Now, however, the Industrial Commission decided to abandon this policy in an effort to obtain deposits.

The Bank Act made ample provision for this new depar-

[1] Figures taken from the monthly bank statements in the *Bank of North Dakota Bulletins.*

[2] *The Bank of North Dakota,* p. 51.

[3] *Ibid.*, p. 51.

ture. Section 9 of the Bank Act reads in part: "The Bank of North Dakota may receive deposits from any . . . domestic individual. . . . Funds may be deposited to the credit of the Bank of North Dakota in any bank or agency approved by the Industrial Commission." Accordingly, on February 18 the Industrial Commission issued an order in which it rehearsed the many expressions of popular favor that the idea of individual deposits had evoked from the citizens of North Dakota from time to time, and feeling that the time was now ripe for such action, it passed resolutions to the effect "that from and after the 21st day of February, 1921 the management of the Bank of North Dakota be instructed to receive time deposits of any and all kinds of either private or public funds together with such checking accounts as can be conveniently handled for depositors."[1] It was then pointed out that, because of the apparently concerted efforts on the part of the privately owned banks in the state to detract from their embarrassment by refusing to cash checks drawn by the Bank of North Dakota or on it, it would therefore be necessary to provide branches at which depositors could carry on their business with the Bank of North Dakota.

Therefore . . . it [was] further resolved that the management of the Bank of North Dakota make immediate arrangements for the establishment of representative agencies or depositories, one or more in each county of the State, which will handle checks or bills of exchange and negotiable paper for collection, deposit, credit or remittance in which the Bank of North Dakota, its depositors or patrons have an interest. That such arrangements be completed at the earliest possible date and that thereupon the Bank of North Dakota receive and accept checking as well as time deposits of both public and private

[1] Order no. 10, Series 1921.

funds from any citizen, corporation or institution inside or outside the State of North Dakota; and that the Bank is authorized to pay on both such time and checking accounts within the State the same rates of interest as now are being paid on public funds deposited in the Bank.[1]

A few days later the Bank sent circulars throughout the state inviting private deposits. These could be made either in person or by mail. The state would guarantee such deposits. Checks, drafts or money orders received for deposit would be credited at par, and payments made to depositors would be free of exchange. Interest would be allowed on these deposits according to the following schedule. On deposits subject to check, the balance not falling below $200 during the month, two per cent would be paid; on balances not falling below $300, two and one-half per cent; on balances not falling below $500, three per cent. Six months' time deposits would receive four and one-half per cent, and twelve months' time deposits five and one-half per cent. In the same circular public treasurers within the state were offered four per cent on time deposits (sinking funds) left four months. On other time deposits, whatever the source, if left six months, four and one-half per cent; if left twelve months, five per cent.[2]

This new banking venture apparently bore little fruit to begin with. The following table shows the fluctuations of individual deposits during the period:[3]

[1] Order no. 10, Series 1921.

[2] *The Bank of North Dakota*, p. 59; *Wall Street Journal*, March 16, 1921; *Financial Age*, April 2, 1921.

[3] Figures taken from monthly bank statements in *Bank of North Dakota Bulletins*.

January 15	$229,039.10
February 16	245,156.56
March 16	258,494.70
April 15	247,037.32
May 16	610,269.77
June 16	641,065.71
July 16	542,426.99
August 16	566,206.63
September 16	576,466.57
October 15	598,527.39
November 15	573,950.36

From the table it appears that it was not until May that the individual deposits grew noticeably. In that month there appeared a remarkable increase; and in the succeeding months individual deposits were maintained at a comparatively high level.

The source of these individual deposits requires comment, for a bank which is undergoing such invidious criticism, to say nothing of the impending necessity to register demand checks for future payment, is not usually sought out by individuals or organizations as a depositary for their funds. Who, then, were the depositors who responded to the drive for individual deposits? The new depositors were individuals and organizations that sympathized with the Bank and the Nonpartisan program, and were willing if need be to suffer inconvenience rather than see the experiment fail.[1]

But the measure of relief from this source was neither important nor dependable. Sound and permanent aid could come to the Bank only if it could thaw out the public funds

[1] *The Fargo Courier-News*, August 4, 1921, reports that the "Public Ownership League of America through its members, agencies and co-operating bodies has handled more than $400,000 worth of business for the State of North Dakota. Over $70,000 worth of bonds have been sold, the balance being in deposits and checking accounts in the Bank of North Dakota." On the following day the *Fargo Courier-News* reported the Amalgamated Garment Workers of Chicago as having deposited $25,000 in the Bank of North Dakota during the past week.

it had frozen in farm loans and other permanent investments in state projects. The Bank would not really be in a healthy condition until the bonds were sold and these loans carried by investors seeking long-time securities. The State Administration and Bank officials realized this fact, and, therefore, put forth every effort to sell the bonds.

BOND SALES

The sale of the various issues of state bonds had, from the first, been a burning question. Mention has already been made of the several futile attempts at getting them properly marketed. Up to the conference of Minneapolis bankers in the middle of January, 1921, the state officials had hoped to market the bonds through the regular financial channels. However, when it appeared that this conference would, like all the rest, result in nothing, announcement was made for the first time that owing to a conspiracy on the part of bond houses and financial interests not to buy North Dakota bonds, this method of marketing them would be abandoned and the state would offer the bonds directly to the investing public.[1] Immediately a vigorous advertising campaign was begun. Aside from the customary monthly bank statement, the entire February bank bulletin was given over to a description of North Dakota bonds, and the security behind them. The bulletin has very much the appearance of the announcements of bond houses having for sale similar issues of public corporation securities. Early in February the Bank of North Dakota sent out a circular letter to the citizens of the state urging them to buy bonds. The circular stated that "The cooperation of the people of North Dakota is solicited to the end that the high financial standing, and integrity of the state may

[1] *Fargo Courier-News*, January 23, 1921.

be sustained." [1] About the middle of April, Attorney General Lemke and Carl D. Thompson, secretary of the Public Ownership League of America, began a tour of the East, holding meetings and conferences in the leading cities for the purpose of organizing committees and in other ways facilitating the sale of the North Dakota bonds.[2] Apparently they had no difficulty in finding plenty of people who sympathized with the cause they represented. It is reported that not only labor and farm organizations endorsed the movement and aided in the sale of bonds, but churches, newspapers and magazines rallied to the support of the bond-selling campaign. Nationally known ministers, editors, mayors, governors, social workers, and reformers became actively engaged in the cause. The Chicago bond-selling campaign was started just after the middle of April, when a regular agency was established.[3] While well organized committees undertook the work of selling the North Dakota bonds in many cities, New York was the only other city in which the State Administration established regular offices.

In a proclamation of July 1, Governor Frazier designated July 23, 1921 as North Dakota Bond Selling Day. In the proclamation he urged " that every public spirited citizen buy as many of the bonds as possible and assist in promoting their sale to others." On July 12 he appealed to the Women's Nonpartisan Clubs " to throw themselves into the campaign and to do all in their power to make North Dakota Bond Selling Day a sweeping success for the farmer-labor industrial program." [4] On July 14 the executive committee

[1] Quoted from circular letter as reported in *Fargo Courier-News*, February 8, 1921.

[2] *Fargo Courier-News*, April 26, 1921.

[3] *Ibid.*, April 20, 26, 1921.

[4] *Fargo Courier-News*, July 13, 1921.

of the Nonpartisan Clubs adopted a resolution urging "the clubs and county federations to do all within their power to further the sale of the bonds." Local and county meetings were urged. "Systematic canvassing" should be resorted to. And the resolution ended with the dramatic assertion that "this is a Liberty Bond sale, as the cause which it represents is a struggle for industrial and economic freedom." [1] The bonds were now offered on the installment plan. Anyone could purchase a bond by paying ten per cent down and the balance in October.[2] This plan would make it possible for the North Dakotans to buy in July and pay for the bonds after threshing.

The *Fargo Courier-News* of August 16 reported the results of the campaign as follows:

> Reports from the Bank of North Dakota indicate that nearly $2,000,000 of bonds were sold in North Dakota on July 23, the day set aside by Gov. Lynn J. Frazier for a special bond drive in this state. As most of these bonds were sold on the installment plan, only part of the money has been received to date.

In the same article it is stated that it was expected that the bond sales would pass the $5,000,000 mark in a few weeks.[3]

To return now briefly to the political developments of the summer, it is worthy of record that the Independent Voters Association, commonly known as the I. V. A., in addition to its relentless warfare on the Bank of North Dakota and North Dakota bond sales, had been circulating petitions for

[1] *Fargo Courier-News*, July 15, 1921.

[2] *Ibid.*, July 23, 1921.

[3] In the *Fargo Courier-News* of October 26 we read, ". . . the $901,753 worth of real estate and mill and elevator bonds which the Forum admits we have sold direct to investors . . . ." Evidently the reports of August were considerably overdrawn.

the recall of the Industrial Commission. On September 16 Secretary of State Thomas Hall

certified to the Governor that petitions had been filed in his office containing the names of 73,893 qualified voters for the recall of Governor Lynn J. Frazier, also petitions with 73,237 names for the recall of Attorney General William Lemke and petitions with 73,187 names for the recall of Commissioner of Agriculture and Labor John Hagan.[1]

Accordingly Secretary Hall fixed October 28, 1921 as the date for the recall election. The late summer and autumn then witnessed an intensified continuation of the activities of the spring and early summer. The I. V. A. continued more vigorously than ever to implicate the Bank and discredit the Industrial Commission. The Industrial Commission and Bank officials with equal vigor attempted to put the Bank into solvent condition and defend their management of the state's industrial program. Needless to say, the fight was exceedingly bitter. The Bank of North Dakota scored a real triumph when on September 26 it was able to announce that it was ready to pay all registered checks, which according to the Bank statement of September 15 amounted to $179,692.84.[2] The Industrial Commission gained further advantage every time it was able to announce notable progress in the sale of bonds. This was particularly true when on October 3 announcement was made that several million dollars worth of bonds had been sold to Spitzer, Rorick & Co. of Toledo, and because of this the Bank would resume the granting of farm loans in the near future.[3]

But the resourceful I. V. A. now executed one of its most spectacular maneuvers. On October 18, 1921, Judge J. A.

[1] *Fargo Courier-News*, September 17, 1921.

[2] *Ibid.*, September 28, 1921.

[3] *Ibid.*, October 4, 1921.

Coffey of the Stutsman County District Court issued a temporary injunction against the Bank and state officials, so sweeping in its orders that, if obeyed, the Bank's hands would have been completely tied, as well as those of the state government.

The action was brought by seventeen plaintiffs "on behalf of themselves and all other taxpayers of North Dakota." [1] The defendants in the action were the members of the Industrial Commission, the State Board of Auditors, the Board of University and School Lands, the Auditing Board of the state, the State Board of Equalization, as well as all the other important state and Bank officials.

In brief, the order prohibited any treasurer from depositing public funds in the Bank of North Dakota, and the Bank officials were enjoined from accepting either private or public funds for deposit. The state governor, secretary, treasurer and auditor were enjoined and restrained from "preparing for issue, signing, sealing and indorsing any bonds upon property of state owned utilities, enterprises or industries." Spitzer, Rorick & Co. were restrained and enjoined "from selling . . . any bonds now in their possession or that may hereafter be delivered to them by or thru any of the defendants." The tax commissioner was "restrained . . . from issuing any orders in respect to the state tax levy so far as it relates to any bonds issued upon property of state owned utilities, enterprises, or industries." [2] The Industrial Commission and Director General Cathro were "restrained . . . from disbursing any funds in the possession, custody and control of the Bank . . . other than for the purpose of paying checks or drafts drawn thereon by bonafide depositors." [3] The Bank of North

[1] *Fargo Courier-News*, October 19, 1921.

[2] *Ibid.*, October 19, 1921.

[3] *Ibid.*, October 19, 1921.

Dakota was "restrained . . . from representing itself as a bank or as a corporation." [1] Finally, the Bank was "adjudged to be insolvent." [2]

On October 20 the supreme court issued an order dissolving the temporary injunction brought by Judge Coffey,[3] and the Nonpartisan Industrial Commission and the Bank of North Dakota went to the polls with final statements in the press that North Dakota bonds to the amount of $6,100,000 had been sold; that Spitzer, Rorick & Co. would be able to take real estate bonds even faster than they could be issued; that all so-called frozen loans made by the Bank were now thawed out; and that if the State Administration and Bank of North Dakota were given a clean bill of health at the recall election, the Bank would "at once be in a position to make farm loans as fast as application [could] be examined and approved." [4]

THE RECALL ELECTION OF OCTOBER, 1921

The recall election, in behalf of which the entire citizenry were to a greater or lesser degree toiling, some to vindicate the Administration, others to repudiate it, meant widely different things to the various people concerned. To those who were sympathetic with the Nonpartisan movement, it represented, in the main, an attempt to overthrow the farmers' program, and the return to power of the "interests". To the opposition it meant various things. To Nestos, the Independent candidate for governor, it meant the turning out of an inefficient, extravagant, if not dishonest set of officials, important changes in some of the Nonpartisan legislation relative to putting the Nonpartisan program into

[1] *Fargo Courier-News*, October 19, 1921.

[2] *Ibid.*, October 19, 1921.

[3] *Ibid.*, October 21, 1921 gives the entire order.

[4] *Ibid.*, October 26, 1921.

effect, but no particular change in the scope of the program.[1] To others of the opposition the whole Nonpartisan program was offensive, and nothing short of its complete annihilation would satisfy them. Thus the *Fargo Forum*, one of the leading opposition dailies of the state, in an editorial on April 7, 1921 made plain the issues as it conceived them.

No recall election which merely means a change in management of the state's industries should be tolerated for a moment by the independent voters of the state. What is wanted and is needed is a receivership for the industries, not just new managers. . . . By all means let us get the issue clear and understand fully that this is a campaign for a receivership for our bankrupt experiment in state socialism and that we are not just fighting to put in another gang of office holders to carry along the experiment.

Besides the recall election of the governor, attorney general and commissioner of agriculture and labor there were three constitutional amendments and six initiated measures to be voted on. Of these, one constitutional amendment and four initiated measures are of interest in a history of the Bank of North Dakota. The constitutional amendment had to do with the amount of state bonds that could be issued to carry out the industrial program. It proposed to reduce the bonded debt limit of the state for that purpose from $12,000,000 to $7,750,000, a sum believed to be sufficient to re-

[1] The *Fargo Courier-News*, April 14, 1921, reports a speech delivered by Mr. Nestos at Minot on April 13, 1921 in which he expressed himself as follows: "As long as the experimentation could be kept within reasonable limits [it] was owing to the farmers of the state who desired these experiments made that the projects already started should be completed, and that they be managed by efficient persons interested in their success."

The *Fargo Courier-News* reports that in the same speech he advocated the continuance of the Bank of North Dakota as an asset to the farmers of the state for the efficient handling of the Rural Credits problem.

organize the several industrial ventures of the state and put them on a sound financial basis.[1]

The measures to be voted on which are of interest here were:[2]

1. Petition for the initiation of a Public Depositary Law.
2. Petition for the initiation of a law to amend and re-enact the Industrial Commission Law.
3. Petition for the initiation of a Rural Credits Law.
4. Petition for the initiation of an act for the dissolution of the Bank of North Dakota.

The substance of the first measure was a disqualification of the Bank of North Dakota for receiving any public deposits whatsoever. Section 4 of the proposed law reads in part as follows:[3]

Any state bank duly incorporated in this state under and pursuant to the laws governing the incorporation of banking corporations, and any national bank situated and doing busi-

[1] *North Dakota Publicity Pamphlet*, October, 1921. It was proposed that section 182 of the North Dakota Constitution be amended so as to read in part as follows:

"The state may issue bonds provided that all bonds issued exceeding in amount a total of Seven Million Seven Hundred Fifty Thousand Dollars ($7,750,000.00), par value, shall be secured by first mortgages upon real estate in amounts not exceeding one-half of the value thereof . . . which bonds [the $7,750,000] may be issued and sold for the following purposes only:

Bonds of the par value not exceeding $5,000,000.00, the proceeds to be used in payment of the debts and liabilities of the Bank of North Dakota;

Bonds of the par value not exceeding $2,500,000, the proceeds to be used to pay the debts and liabilities of the North Dakota Mill and Elevator Association, to pay the expense of completing the state owned mill and elevator at Grand Forks, and as working capital for the operation of such mill and elevator;

Bonds of the total par value not exceeding $250,000, the proceeds to be used in payment of the debts and liabilities of the North Dakota Home Building Association."

[2] *North Dakota Publicity Pamphlet*, October, 1921.

[3] *Ibid.*

ness within the State of North Dakota may be designated a depository of public funds. . . .

This, of course, leaves the Bank of North Dakota out of consideration.

The second measure is of interest here mainly because of its implications. If this measure became law the Industrial Commission was to be revised, apparently in such a way as to jeopardize the Bank even though the other measures which were leveled directly at it failed to become law.[1] The measure was so drafted as to ignore the existence of the Bank. It is a matter of conjecture what would have happened had this measure been enacted into law, while the measures designed to destroy the Bank failed.

The third measure was designed to create a board to take over the farm-loan business of the Bank in case it were dissolved; or if the measure providing for the Bank's dissolution failed to become law, to withdraw the farm-loan business and put it into the hands of a "Rural Credits Board".

Finally, there was a measure whose purpose can best be described by quoting its first section.[2]

That the Bank of North Dakota as established and created by Chapter 147 of the Session Laws of 1919 be and the same is hereby discontinued and dissolved for all purposes except for the purpose of liquidation, as herewith provided.

The measure provided for the creation of a board of trustees for the dissolution of the Bank, and lest any time be lost in disposing of the odious State Bank, section 12 was made to read, "This act is hereby declared to be an

[1] The Nonpartisans realized this and called attention to it in their criticism of the I. V. A. program in the *North Dakota Publicity Pamphlet*, October, 1921.

[2] *North Dakota Publicity Pamphlet*, October, 1921.

emergency measure and shall take effect and be in force from and after its passage and approval."

Thus, to repeat, the State Bank was both directly and indirectly to be held up to the people for vindication or for dissolution in the October 28 election. Small wonder that the fight centered almost exclusively around its management and condition.

RECALL ELECTION RETURNS

The official returns of the October 28 election gave to the Independent candidate for governor, Rangvold A. Nestos, a majority of 4,102; to the Independent candidate for attorney general, Sveinbjorn Johnson, a majority of 6,786; and to the Independent candidate for commissioner of agriculture and labor, Joseph A. Kitchen, a majority of 5,335. Thus the Nonpartisan Industrial Commission was recalled and a new Independent Industrial Commission elected. The constitutional amendment and initiated measures briefly described above failed to command the necessary number of votes, the official returns showing that they lost by narrow margins.[1]

The election of the Independent candidates for the important state offices with the rejection of their platform at the same election made the desiderata of the people of North Dakota somewhat obscure. There were those who believed that the repudiation of the Independent platform meant that the people wanted none of the Independent campaign promises fulfilled. Others claimed that it was a mandate to the new Industrial Commission to carry on the Nonpartisan program in the same manner as had the Nonpartisan Industrial Commission.[2] Governor-elect Nestos interpreted the

[1] *Farmer-Labor State Record* (Bismarck), December 1, 1921.

[2] From Governor-elect Nestos' speech at the I. V. A. Victory Celebration at Devil's Lake, November 4, 1921, as reported in the *Fargo Courier-News*, November 6, 1921.

election to mean that the people of the state endorsed the new Industrial Commission's campaign promises and elected its members believing that they would carry them out. And this he proposed to do, even though the laws and administrative machinery with which he had to work were not exactly to his fancy.[1]

The newly elected members of the Industrial Commission were to assume office November 23. In the meantime the recalled Industrial Commission continued to function and events of considerable importance to the Bank took place. The widely heralded bond sale to Spitzer, Rorick & Co. of Toledo, called for the delivery of real estate bonds about as soon as they could be prepared. On November 2 the Administration encountered an obstacle when Secretary of State Thomas Hall refused to sign any more real estate bonds.[2] On November 10 Judge W. L. Nuessle in district court issued an order restraining further delivery of state bonds by the Bank of North Dakota to the Toledo bond company. Members of the Industrial Commission as well as F. W. Cathro, manager of the Bank, were included in the order. Taxpayers alleging that the bonds were being sold below par in violation of the law had made the complaint on which the order was issued.

The facts in the case were these. The Bank of North Dakota contracted with Spitzer, Rorick & Co. of Toledo for the sale of bonds to the amount of $6,100,000 at discounts of five, four and two per cent on various issues. The Industrial Commission sold the bonds to the Bank at par. The Bank in turn sold them to the bond house at the discounts mentioned above.[3] The state contended that in this

[1] *Ibid.*

[2] *Fargo Courier-News*, November 3, 1921.

[3] *Ibid.*, November 11, 19, 1921. Also from Mr. Cathro's affidavit filed in the Burleigh County District Court reported in full in the *Fargo Courier-News*, November 16, 1921.

manner the law had been complied with. The complaining taxpayers claimed that the order was nothing but a subterfuge to avoid the law. Attorney General William Lemke for the state and G. G. Kehoe for the taxpayers agreed on Judge A. T. Cole of Fargo to try the case. However it was agreed by the attorneys and approved by Judge Cole that the case go directly to the state supreme court.[1] A few days later, and before any decision was rendered in the case, announcement was made that the Industrial Commission had signed a new contract with Spitzer, Rorick & Co., replacing the old one which was under fire in the state supreme court. This contract included all the remaining authorized bond issues and provided that all bonds not yet issued should be sold at par. The issues included in the contract were as follows:

Real Estate series	$8,000,000
Mill and Elevator series	2,000,000
Home Builders Association bonds	1,000,000
Bank of North Dakota bonds	1,300,000

In order to sell the real estate bonds at par it was necessary to increase the rate of interest on them from five and three-quarters to six per cent. The five per cent Bank bonds were sold at a discount to net five and five eighths per cent.[2]

The announcement of this new sale was made on November 22, the day before the new administration was to take office. According to Attorney General Lemke, the signing of this contract brought the total amount of bonds sold by the outgoing Industrial Commission up to approximately $15,000,000.[3]

Thus ended one of the most sensational chapters in banking history. This hectic and turbulent period wrought im-

[1] *Fargo Courier-News*, November 19, 1921.

[2] *Ibid.*, November 23, 1921.

[3] *Ibid.*

portant changes in the Bank's condition. These may best be shown by placing side by side the items of the Bank's statements for October 15, 1920 and November 23, 1921. The reader may then make his own comparisons and form his own conclusions. The items follow: [1]

RESOURCES

	October 15, 1920	*November 23, 1921*
Bonds, United States, State and County	$1,984,522.50	$1,072,791.93
Loans to Banks	2,507,323.90	1,902,513.50
Loans to Public Institutions and Departments	450,000.00	1,580,615.77
Loans on Warehouse Receipts	119,277.00	53,980.42
Loans on Real Estate	2,905,335.00	330,707.39
Interest Earned (Net) and Uncollected	268,479.18	215,362.07
Furniture and Fixtures	48,834.92	52,673.67
Due from 814 (Oct., 1920) and 208 (Nov., 1921) Depositary Banks in North Dakota (Redeposit)	8,871,436.72	2,118,244.82
Due from Correspondent Banks Outside of North Dakota	586,616.14	1,513,114.94
Collection Items due from Banks in the State	1,652,809.78	236,697.59
Collection Items due from the State and Public Corporations	76,692.00	320,231.27
Cash on Hand and Cash Items	55,380.99	113,992.86
Contingent Fund (State Treasurer's Registered Checks)	None	259.19
State Treasurer: Farm Loans delivered for Bond Issue	None	2,568,333.85
Total Resources	$19,526,708.13	$10,339,284.68

[1] *Bank of North Dakota Bulletin*, October, 1920; *Fargo Courier-News*, December 11, 1921.

LIABILITIES

	October 15, 1920	*November 23, 1921*
Capital	$2,000,000.00	$2,000,000.00
Surplus	40,000.00	40,000.00
Reserve to Repay Legislative Appropriation	23,954.10	None
Reserve for Depreciation on Furniture and Fixtures	7,805.34	16,913.98
Net Profits	103,178.66	167,038.61
Appraisal Fees (On Hand)	4,225.36	4,031.13
Public Deposits, Sinking Fund	3,400,855.40	1,380,413.32
Public Deposits, General and Other Funds	10,752,287.60	4,520,888.48
Individual Deposits	189,027.35	1,502,204.38
Bills Payable	1,000,000.00	None
Collection Items	None	2,688.56
Due to Depositary Banks (Reserves)	2,005,374.32	263,922.00
Cashier's Checks	None	20,269.88
Registered Checks	None	10,885.65
Proceeds of Bonds	None	410,028.69
Total Liabilities	$19,526,708.13	$10,339,284.68

The diminution of the footings by about fifty per cent is notable. This meant that the volume of the Bank's business had been halved. The cause of this tremendous shrinkage can easily be traced to the great diminution of the public deposits and bank reserve funds carried by the state banks in the Bank of North Dakota. So great was the falling away of these deposits that the remarkable increase in the amount of individual deposits was powerless to keep the total deposits from shrinking to less than half their former amount.

But while the Bank suffered this contraction in the volume of its business, forces were at work to strengthen that which remained. Especially notable is the great improvement in the proportion of cash held. In spite of the fact that deposits were less than forty-seven per cent of their amount in October, 1920, yet cash holdings were double the amount then held. The smaller sum tied up in bonds also evidences improvement and the statement shows that more than two and a half millions were about to be released from the farm loans through funds obtained by the bonds actually sold. The reader can, by examining the above figures, find further evidence of an improved condition. The Bank had passed a crisis. The battle that it had waged with its adversaries had stripped it of much of its potentiality. But that same struggle had accomplished untold good for the Bank in pruning out much of the error which had sprung up in its less contentious days. It is interesting to speculate on what the Bank's future might have been had the recall election failed to remove the Nonpartisan Administration. Would the lesson of 1921 have served to usher in a wiser policy in the Bank's administration, or would the same errors have been committed again as soon as the critics had been silenced? It is impossible to answer such a question. Those who believe that a government can operate a business enterprise as wisely and economically as private individuals, will answer that the experience gained would have made possible the operation of the Bank in a most satisfactory manner. Those to whom government operation of business is distasteful will reply that it is not the lack of experience but of fidelity that causes failures in government business. The recall election results prevented the test from being made in North Dakota.

THE NONPARTISAN INDUSTRIAL COMMISSION RETIRES

The change in the Bank's administration was now at hand. On November 22 the outgoing members of the Industrial Commission unanimously adopted a resolution urging those who had thus far supported the Bank to continue that support under the new administration, and expressing their faith that if the Bank were thus supported it would be a great success and a benefit to the people of North Dakota.[1] On November 23 the recalled members of the Industrial Commission gave way to the three men who were elected to replace them.

As Governor Frazier was leaving the Capitol he gave out a message in which he thanked those who had supported him during his stormy administration, and assured all that he was leaving office "with malice toward none". Expressing regret that he had not been able to render greater service, and further expressing his faith in the ultimate victory of the industrial program, he took occasion to say, "We have left the Bank of North Dakota, the keystone of the Program, in splendid financial shape for our successor to use, and I sincerely hope he will be able to immediately aid our hardly pressed farmers." [2]

Late in the afternoon Rangvold A. Nestos was sworn in as governor of North Dakota. At the same time Sveinbjorn Johnson and Joseph A. Kitchen assumed the offices of attorney general and commissioner of agriculture and labor. These three men formed the new Industrial Commission. The Bank of North Dakota had been delivered into the hands of its former enemies.

[1] *Fargo Courier-News*, November 23, 1921.

[2] *Ibid.*, November 24, 1921.

CHAPTER VII

The Bank of North Dakota Under the Independent Administration

In the preceding chapter mention was made of the fact that in the ranks of the I. V. A. could be found all shades of beliefs and opinions from those held by "bitter-enders", whom nothing short of complete annihilation of the whole state industrial program would satisfy, to those held by more moderate citizens who believed that the program should be given a trial, but on a conservative scale and under honest and efficient management. Fortunately for the Bank, Governor Nestos was of those who counseled moderation and believed that the program should be given a fair trial. Moreover, while he would have preferred the Rural Credits System which was defeated at the recall election, yet he was not entirely out of sympathy with the Bank of North Dakota. In his inaugural address he commented on the Bank Law as follows: [1]

> I feet . . . that an efficient and economical system of rural credits can be established and conducted under the present laws of our state and will result in securing for the farmers of our state the privilege of making farm loans at a reasonable rate of interest and at small cost. Such defects as exist in the present law can be obviated and the public interest fully safeguarded by regulations to be adopted by the new industrial commission.

[1] *Fargo Courier-News*, November 24, 1921. Doubtless the second word in the quotation is a typographical error and should be *feel*.

The new governor's principal objections to the Bank were those dealing with faulty policies and management. These he proposed to remedy. But aside from that there would be no important change. The Bank of North Dakota was to continue to operate along the lines on which it was already functioning. Special emphasis would be laid on the rural credits feature.[1] Its management would be more conservative.

NEW BANK OFFICERS

When the new Industrial Commission sought another director general for the Bank, W. B. DeNault was looked upon with favor for the position. Mr. DeNault lived in Jamestown, had practical mortgage banking experience, and had been put in charge of the farm-loan department of the Bank of North Dakota on December 1. When he was approached by the Industrial Commission with an offer to act in the dual capacity of director general and head of the farm-loan department, he declined to assume this double responsibility. It was decided, therefore, that he should remain in the farm-loan department and build up this most important branch of the Bank's service. DeNault had a good conservative mortgage banking record. The Governor expressed the belief that he would develop the real estate loan business of the State Bank on similarly sound and conservative principles.[2]

Upon Mr. DeNault's refusal C. R. Green of Cavalier was elected by the Industrial Commission to be the successor of Director General Cathro. Green had been in the banking business in North Dakota for more than twenty-five years, had been president of the North Dakota Bankers' Association and, when appointed director general of the State Bank,

[1] *Fargo Courier-News*, November 6, 1921.

[2] *Ibid.*, December 2, 1921.

was a member of its executive council. Cathro's judgment of the appointment was expressed in a statement to the press in which he referred to Green as being "cautious, deliberate and conservative in regard to specific transactions that come before him for decisions, but progressive as . . . to general development and advancement."[1] The selection indeed met so thoroughly with the retired Nonpartisan director general's approval that he warmly urged the people of the state to put their confidence in the new administration.

FARM LOAN BUSINESS REORGANIZED

The farm-loan department commended itself for further development more than any other department of the Bank. The Industrial Commission gave it their immediate attention, and Mr. DeNault shortly worked out a scheme whereby a farmer who received a loan on his land from the Bank could amortize the principal in twenty-six years. The necessity of having the entire loan repaid within that time lay in the wording of section 4 of the Real Estate Bond Act. The law required that the real estate bonds be repaid "in not less than ten or more than thirty years from the passage of [the] Act." As nearly three years had elapsed since the act had been passed and the loans would have to be made largely during the fourth year, and the bonds then issued, Mr. DeNault based his plan on a twenty-six year basis. The plan which he worked out, and which was approved by the Industrial Commission follows. The table assumes a $1000 loan.[2]

It will be seen that this plan called for an interest rate of six and one-half per cent. However, when the payment on principal was included it was the equivalent of eight per cent on the original amount of the loan. This, however, automatically amortized the principal.

[1] *Fargo Courier-News*, January 1, 1922.

[2] *Ibid.*, January 4, 1922.

Payment Number	Year	Interest	Principal	Amount Unpaid
1	1923	$65.00	$15.00	$985.00
2	1924	64.03	15.97	969.03
3	1925	62.99	17.01	952.02
4	1926	61.88	18.12	933.90
5	1927	60.70	19.30	914.60
6	1928	59.45	20.55	894.05
7	1929	58.11	21.89	872.16
8	1930	56.69	23.31	848.85
9	1931	55.17	24.83	824.02
10	1932	53.56	26.44	797.58
11	1933	51.48	28.16	769.42
12	1934	50.01	29.99	739.43
13	1935	48.07	31.93	707.50
14	1936	45.99	34.01	673.49
15	1937	43.78	36.22	637.27
16	1938	41.42	38.58	598.69
17	1939	38.91	41.09	557.60
18	1940	36.24	43.79	513.84
19	1941	33.40	46.60	467.24
20	1942	30.37	49.63	417.61
21	1943	27.14	52.86	364.75
22	1944	23.71	56.29	308.46
23	1945	20.05	59.95	248.51
24	1946	16.15	63.85	184.66
25	1947	12.00	68.00	116.66
26	1948	7.58	116.66	——

APPRAISALS OF FORMER ADMINISTRATION DECLARED VOID

Another part of the farm-loan business to engage the attention of the department was the matter of farm appraisals. Mr. Frank E. Currey of Finley, N. D., an employee of the Federal Land Bank of St. Paul, was temporarily loaned to the Bank of North Dakota and put in charge of the appraisals for new loans.[1] This work assumed additional importance when the Bank declared that all the old appraisals which were carried over from the former administration were void. The reasons given for this departure were that

[1] *Fargo Courier-News*, January 28, 1922.

many of the appraisals were as much as two years old, that conditions had changed much, and that the Bank was therefore not warranted in making loans on the basis of such appraisals.[1]

PREPARATION FOR THE RESUMPTION OF LOANING

The Bank began to send the new farm-loan applications to bankers and individuals on January 9,[2] and on January 27 Director DeNault announced that the department was ready to make loans.[3]

THE BANK ANTICIPATES A HANDICAP

Since the Frazier Administration had made loans to the amount of $2,760,331.83 there remained $7,239,668.17 to be loaned before the $10,000,000 provided by law would be exhausted.[4] In view of this limitation the Industrial Com-

[1] *Fargo Courier-News*, February 4, 1922

The rejection of these old appraisals it has been charged, was for a sinister purpose. Thus William Langer, former Attorney General of North Dakota, in a speech at Underwood, N. D. on June 5, 1922 charged that Nestos and DeNault dumped nearly $4,000,000 worth of applications aside on pretext that they had been appraised too high when as a matter of fact only a very few might have been. The object, according to Langer, was that Nestos did not want the Bank to function and would do all he could to prevent it. Langer viewed the appointment of "experienced appraisers" in the form of bankers and those who had experience in farm-mortgage business as part of the Nestos program of sabotaging the Bank. For these men who had business connections with financial institutions whom the Bank of North Dakota would compete against could be depended upon to under-appraise land and thus drive the desperate farmer into the jaws of the private banker and loan shark. Langer charged that he had uncovered a conspiracy on the part of the Nestos Administration and Minneapolis financial interests to sabotage the Bank.—See the *Fargo Courier-News*, June 6, 1922.

[2] *Condensed Statement of the Condition of the Bank of North Dakota*, March 10, 1922.

[3] *Fargo Courier-News*, January 28, 1922.

[4] *Report of the North Dakota Industrial Commission*, 1922, p. 18.

mission, on February 27, adopted a resolution indorsing the proposal of the State Administration for an initiated law to be submitted to the June primary which would multiply the usefulness of the farm-loan department by raising the real estate bond limit from $10,000,000 to $20,000,000. This sum, it was thought, would take care of all the loans the department could make before the legislature, convening in January, 1923, could provide for further expansion.[1]

AVAILABLE FUNDS ALLOTTED TO COUNTIES

In order to apportion the available funds with fairness, the Industrial Commission limited individual loans to $8000 and DeNault worked out a system of allotments to the various counties in the state. The allotment was on the basis of .0095 per cent of the 1921 assessed valuation of the land in each county. The counties were classified into four groups. Those in the western part of the state comprising district number one were allotted 200 per cent of the base; those in district number two, 150 per cent of the base; those in district number three, the base; and those in district number four, the Red River Valley, one-half the base per cent of the assessed valuation.[2] A table giving the allotments to the several counties together with other germane figures follows.[3]

[1] *Fargo Courier-News*, February 28, 1922.

[2] *Report of the North Dakota Industrial Commission*, 1922, p. 19.

In the second $10,000,000 made available by initiated law the allotment was the same except that the counties Burke, Divide, Mountrail, Renville, Ward and Williams of the second district were included under the first district allotment base rate.

[3] *Condensed Statement of the Condition of the Bank of North Dakota*, March 10, 1922.

County	Allotment	Loans made by former administration	Funds available for new loans	New applications received up to 3-11-22
Adams	$98,000	$42,490.00	$55,510.00	$92,900
Barnes	192,000	3,960.00	188,040.00	112,900
Benson	180,000	10,408.00	169,592.00	291,000
Billings	79,000	27,753.00	51,247.00	90,000
Bottineau	234,000	242,512.00	....	27,000
Bowman	102,000	42,520.00	59,480.00	103,300
Burke	144,000	59,898.00	84,102.00	161,700
Burleigh	299,000	322,136.31	....	12,800
Cass	291,000	....	271,000.00	54,500
Cavalier	166,000	8,910.00	147,090.00	159,300
Dickey	227,000	3,960.00	223,040.00	72,000
Divide	135'000	49,020.00	85,980.00	380,650
Dunn	233,000	114,185.00	118,815.00	329,550
Eddy	121,000	9,524.00	111,476.00	195,350
Emmons	198,000	48,780.00	149,220.00	278,690
Foster	124,000	3,465.00	120,535.00	93,500
Golden Valley	103,000	80,259.00	22,741.00	44,900
Grand Forks	208,000	31,680.00	176,320.00	113,700
Grant	199,000	74,357.00	124,643.00	307,050
Griggs	92,000	....	92,000.00	139,800
Hettinger	123,000	97,025.40	25,974.60	167,400
Kidder	239,000	110,710.00	128,290.00	116,000
LaMoure	235,000	58,500.00	176,500.00	178,350
Logan	93,000	62,120.00	30,880.00	356,200
McHenry	229,000	157,991.00	71,009.00	187,200
McIntosh	100,000	....	100,000.00	215,800
McKenzie	192,000	38,138.00	153,862.00	383,950
McLean	351,000	94,100.00	256,900.00	552,550
Mercer	154,000	89,000.10	64,999.90	469,000
Morton	267,000	102,544.00	164,456.00	377,750
Mountrail	178,000	20,682.00	157,318.00	225,500
Nelson	121,000	26,400.00	94,600.00	182,600
Oliver	103,000	24,261.00	78,739.00	87,200
Pembina	147,000	36,395.00	110,605.00	142,600
Pierce	113,000	3,870.00	109,130.00	182,225
Ramsey	129,000	8,415.00	120,585.00	125,000
Ransom	103,000	58,155.00	44,845.00	87,200
Renville	121,000	175,546.20	....	22,600
Richland	208,000	....	188,000.00	107,000
Rolette	109,000	13,000.00	96,000.00	153,200
Sargent	89,000	6,673.00	82,327.00	99,800
Sheridan	131,000	33,422.00	97,578.00	125,800
Sioux	36,000	2,178.00	33,822.00	28,500
Slope	114,000	38,342.00	75,658.00	101,000
Stark	167,000	140,227.00	26,773.00	330,450
Steele	93,000	12,000.00	81,000.00	143,200
Stutsman	403,000	78,515.00	324,485.00	365,800
Towner	196,000	4,950.00	191,050.00	90,350
Trail	137,000	4,950.00	112,050.00	90,100
Walsh	191,000	....	174,805.49	81,700
Ward	292,000	51,103.90	240,896.10	262,000
Wells	199,000	....	199,000.00	138,200
Williams	212,000	46,669.00	165,311.00	352,700

In making the allotment a special reserve of one million dollars was set aside to cover emergency cases occurring in any county of the state. This was done in order that no farmer offering a safe loan need lose his land because the allotment to his particular county happened to be exhausted.[1] Emergency cases were deemed to be those where the farmers were in immediate danger of actually losing their land at an early date through the expiration of the year of redemption under foreclosure conducted a year before.[2] Cases where foreclosure had been merely threatened were not considered emergency cases, but, since urgent, were given second consideration. As far as possible the urgency of the case was to determine its preference.[3]

FARMS APPRAISED AND LOANS MADE

Regular appraisals of the farms were first made about February 1. Seven appraisers spent all of their time in the field, and loans were made as rapidly as the office force could digest them. The policy of the department was to appraise and approve loans no faster than they were able to close and pay them. By March 10 the department announced that farms had been appraised in fifty-two of the fifty-three counties in the state and new loans approved to the amount of $271,250. Appraisals were coming in and loans approved at the rate of from $15,000 to $25,000 a

[1] *Fargo Courier-News*, March 10, 1922.

[2] The emergency fund was doubled when $1,000,000 was added from the $10,000,000 made available in June. $877,600 of this fund was used in 1922.

[3] The fact that the Bank offered to give second consideration to cases where foreclosure was threatened served to stimulate creditors to proceed against their debtors. The Bank was forced to disregard such claims, but continued to give "preferred consideration to cases where foreclosures occurred a year ago and where redemption [was] about to expire."—See the *Fargo Courier-News*, April 8, 1922.

day.[1] The first actual closing and paying of loans occurred in March. Seven loans amounting in all to $34,600 were made during the month.

FRICTION DEVELOPS

It will be recalled that when the new administration first assumed the responsibility of running the Bank, a considerable show of harmony was exhibited between the new and the old officials. So also the press, as well as the farmers, appeared for the time being to be sheathing their swords, and the state seemed to be in an attitude of hopeful expectancy with respect to the good that would be accomplished by the Bank under the direction of the new officials. But it was too much to hope that this unexpected lull in the political storm of North Dakota should become a permanent calm. The farm-loan department of the Bank had not been functioning long before the policies of the department were again beginning to meet with disfavor, and here and there disapproval was voiced by press and farmer alike. As the year progressed the first muffled and scattered murmurs of disapproval swelled into a great cry of Nonpartisan farmers, politicians and press denouncing the Nestos Administration's control of the state industries, and particularly the administration of the farm-loan department of the Bank. Many who had been led to hope that under Nestos the Bank of North Dakota would speedily aid in solving the farm-loan dilemma of the state, were sadly disappointed when the Bank did not relieve the situation with dispatch.

REASONS FOR DISSATISFACTION

The storm of protest against the Nestos Administration was raised in first instance because of the very conservative

[1] *Condensed Statement of the Condition of the Bank of North Dakota*, March 10, 1922.

policy of the farm-loan department. The new policy was admittedly conservative. In most cases the new appraisal reduced the amount which the Bank would loan on a farm considerably below the sum permitted by the appraisal discarded by DeNault. New and stricter standards were set up. For instance, while loans were still based primarily on the value of the land offered for security, yet " a farmer showing a good diversification in milk cows, other cattle, hogs and poultry, and in the raising of corn, tame grass and potatoes on his land " would get a somewhat larger loan than those whose operations were not diversified.[1]

As early as March 10 the director of the farm-loan department complained that the Bank was " suffering a substantial delay in the failure on the part of the applicants to move promptly in the matter of accepting the loans approved at reduced amounts." [2] The reason the farmer did not move promptly was because of the shock he suffered when he found out the amount he could borrow from the Bank on his first mortgage and realized its inadequacy for his needs. He must " shop around " and see if in a private mortgage bank he could be better taken care of, onerous though the interest rates might be. Furthermore, the Nonpartisan press complained that the Bank officials did not go out of their way to explain clearly to the farmers that the eight per cent charged on the loan included both interest and amortization charges.[3] Many farmers, it feared, were comparing the eight per cent of the Bank of North Dakota with the eight per cent which a private banker might charge as interest alone.

[1] *Condensed Statement of the Condition of the Bank of North Dakota*, March 10, 1922.

[2] *Ibid.*

[3] *Fargo Courier-News*, March 1, 1922.

SUMMARY OF THE FARM LOAN OPERATIONS—1922

What the Bank of North Dakota accomplished in the way of making farm loans in 1922 may now be presented. Loans, actually closed, are listed in the following table according to the months in which they were made.[1]

January	—	none
February	—	none
March	7	$34,600
April	22	79,750
May	69	214,300
June	74	273,450
July	131	437,750
August	162	494,140
September	144	428,150
October	163	538,051
November	134	438,300
December	170	532,200
Totals for year	1077	$3,470,691

A summary of unclosed loans as of December 31, 1922 is as follows:[2]

In preparation section	$696,950
In title section	196,700
In closing section	1,310,200
Total	$2,204,850

The total number of applications on file on December 31, 1922 was 5,314 requesting loans amounting to $16,485,255.[3] The total number of appraisals made during the year was 3,773.[4]

[1] *Report of the North Dakota Industrial Commission*, 1922, p. 19.

[2] *Ibid.*, p. 19.

[3] *Ibid.*, p. 19.

[4] *Ibid.*, p. 20.

CRITICISM OF FARM LOAN OPERATIONS

It must be noted at this point that a conservative policy of bank management was certain to bring down bitter criticism on the heads of the officials, however justified such a policy might be. However, an examination of the above summary of the farm-loan department's operations for 1922 reveals an unwarranted slowness in making loans.[1] The farmers' need for money was great. Bankruptcies and foreclosures were the order of the day. Yet in the face of this disaster only $3,470,691 were paid out in a year's time. Surely few would have the hardihood to say that this was a creditable showing!

Why did the Bank not make more farm loans in 1922? But two explanations present themselves. One is that the farmers did not care to accept the amount which the new administration offered to loan on their land. The other is that the Bank could not, or would not, digest the loans and close them with dispatch. The situation viewed from either angle has led careful observers both in North Dakota and elsewhere to the conclusion that the Independent Administration has had as its main aim discredit, sabotage and destruction of the Bank. That may be stating the case too strongly. A safe conclusion, however, is that so far under the Independent Administration the Bank of North Dakota has been of little more aid to the farmers in furnishing them with land credit than it was under the Nonpartisan Administration. It appears that conditions were far more favorable for the proper functioning of the farm-loan department in 1922 than ever in the history of the Bank.

[1] Particularly surprising when it is recalled that the Bank officials, early in the year, deplored the fact that they would be so greatly hampered by a $10,000,000 limit. The Industrial Commission adopted a resolution in favor of raising the limit to $20,000,000 in order that the work be not hindered in 1922.

But the record of loans is on the whole unsatisfactory, especially in view of the urgency of the need, and the opportunities for service at hand.

FINANCING THE 1922 CROP

The summer of 1922 revived the spirit of optimism on many North Dakota farms. Weather conditions were favorable. The wheat crop was good. In some sections of the state it was the first that many had harvested in several years. Moreover the price of wheat was fair during the early summer months. As harvest approached there was reason to believe that the farmers would make a profit on their operations.

But the grain was not yet ripe when wheat prices began to decline. During harvest they continued downward, and when threshing began they had touched the lowest levels since 1915. But the bottom had not yet been reached and as the wheat came on the market it forced the price to descend to new low levels. The money return for a good crop was disheartening. Yet many of the farmers had no alternative; their creditors were forcing them to sell on a broken market.

As a rule wheat prices are lower in the Autumn than at any other season of the year. This fact has led some observers to the conclusion that the wheat market is manipulated by speculators in such a manner as to depress the prices when the crop is being sold. It is, however, a mistake to suppose that this is the primary, or even an important cause of the seasonal "slump" in prices. The low price may be fully accounted for by the well-known forces of demand and supply operating in an unmanipulated market. It is of no avail to condemn organized markets and to legislate against future sales of the product. The cause of the seasonal slump lies deeper. Low prices in the Autumn are the result of placing on the market during a few months what it takes a year to consume. The market for wheat is, indeed, a world market. But it is significant that the important wheat fields of the world lie in the Northern Hemisphere and, therefore, their seed-time and harvest correspond with our own.

The depression of the wheat market in the Autumn of 1922 was the natural result of recurring circumstances which the Bank of North Dakota was designed to avert for that state. It had been expected that the Bank would assist the farmers to hold their wheat in case the market broke under the seasonal selling pressure. So, as the market weakened, a cry arose demanding that something be done to save the situation. The Bank Administration was denounced for its apparent indifference to the farmers' plight.

THE FARGO MARKETING CONFERENCE

The Bank officials were, however, fully aware of the gravity of the situation. On September 13 Governor Nestos called a conference of farmers and bankers at Fargo to discuss the problem of marketing the 1922 crop. At the conference it was agreed that proper financing was the most important factor in the problem. One of the members urged that the Bank of North Dakota loan on grain in the farmers' granaries. The governor is said to have replied that the Bank was having a difficult time to finance the farm-loan department and the Grand Forks mill and elevator project, and that it was in no position to borrow money.[1]

[1] *Fargo Courier-News*, September 14, 1922.

It is worth noting that the Governor delivered himself of this statement of the Bank's impotence in less than three weeks after he had, according to an Associated Press report in the *Fargo Courier-News*, August 27, made a statement before the Minneapolis Rotary Club to the effect that steps to dissolve the Bank of North Dakota would be taken at the next legislative session.

After due consideration the finance committee of the conference brought in a resolution in which they expressed their opinion as follows:

We believe there is ample credit now available through the ordinary banking and government channels to market this present crop in an orderly manner and without forcing any worthy producer to dispose of his crop before he desires to do so.[1]

The conference approved this verdict.

CRITICISM

The reasonableness of this resolution may be challenged. " Credit . . .available through . . . Government channels " meant the aid that the War Finance Corporation was extending to the North Dakota Wheat Growers Association. At best it would reach only a small fraction of the farmers. "The ordinary banking . . . channels ", still considerably clogged with over-due loans, were in no position to be of much assistance. On the contrary, the local banks were in most instances the creditors who were responsible for the " forcing ".

The question, Why would not Governor Nestos let the Bank of North Dakota function in furnishing credit to the farmer at this time? deserves attention. There is no doubt that he realized the need for much help. The Fargo Marketing Conference was called to help solve the financing problem. Immediately after this conference the governor made a trip to Washington to plead for more War Finance Corporation money. But never was the Bank of North Dakota to share in the extension of credit to the hard-pressed farmers. "The ordinary banking . . . channels " were to be the means whereby the farmers were, if at all,

[1] *Fargo Courier-News*, September 16, 1922.

to be saved. Did the governor believe that the Bank of North Dakota was in a weaker position than the private banks in the state? Surely a study of comparative bank statistics and statements could not have supported such a belief. Did he believe that the private banks were in a better position to avail themselves of outside help? It may be, for he is credited with the statement that the Bank of North Dakota was in no position to borrow money.

The governor's statement, that the Bank was having difficulties in financing the farm-loan department and the Grand Forks mill and elevator, requires comment.[1] It was surprising to hear that the Bank was having difficulties in financing the farm loans. In February the officials had complained that a ten-million-dollar limit would handicap their operations for the year. At the June primary election they had assisted in raising the limit to twenty millions in the hope that the larger sum would suffice until the legislative assembly of 1923 could provide for further expansion. However, at the time of the Fargo Marketing Conference not more than two million dollars had been loaned on land by the Independent Administration. It is amazing to hear that so small a fraction of the loans which a few months before it had confidently expected to make, was taxing the Bank's resources. Surely some unforeseen obstruction had checked the work of the farm-loan department.

Likewise the financing of the Grand Forks mill and elevator was said to be straining the Bank. This plant was nearing completion in the Autumn of 1922. The first of the three units of the mill began operations on October 30.

As early as March 3, 1922, Lewis F. Crawford, secretary of the Industrial Commission, filed a three-million-dollar mortgage for the Mill and Elevator Association. The mortgage was made to the state of North Dakota and was to be

[1] *Supra*, p. 174.

the basis on which the mill and elevator bonds were to be issued. $1,100,000 of the authorized $3,000,000 mill and elevator bonds were to be issued immediately to provide for the repayment of advances made by the Bank of North Dakota on the Grand Forks enterprise,[1] and for the continuation of the work in the Spring.[2] The remainder of the lot would be issued and sold as required and as the project was completed.

So apparently in this case as in the case of the farm-loan department, the machinery for successfully financing the project was at hand. The Bank's embarrassment was, as under the Frazier Administration, that the bonds were not being sold and the burden of these long-term credits shifted from the shoulders of the Bank to the public seeking long-time investments.[3]

But under the Frazier Administration, it will be remembered, every effort was made in season and out to sell these bonds. The I. V. A. politician never wearied of criticizing the lengths that the Nonpartisans would go in order to sell a bond. Finally, at the close of the Nonpartisan rule a large block of bonds was sold to a bond company, and while a somewhat unfavorable bargain was struck, yet under the circumstances it was a good one for the state.

However, the Nestos Administration's political aggrandizement lay in exactly the opposite direction from that of

[1] At the close of business on March 10, 1922 the Mill and Elevator Association owed the Bank of North Dakota $1,053,310.50 besides interest. This first issue of $1,100,000 was sold to Spitzer, Rorick & Co. under the contract made by the Frazier Administration.

[2] *Fargo Courier-News*, March 4 and February 28, 1922.

[3] According to the 1922 *Report of the North Dakota Industrial Commission*: The contract between Spitzer, Rorick & Co. and the Frazier Administration included the sale of $3,000,000 mill and elevator bonds at six per cent. The contract modified by the Nestos Administration allowed $1,100,000 to go to Spitzer, Rorick & Co. as under the old contract but withheld from sale the other $1,900,000.

Frazier's. The Bank of North Dakota was the child of the political organization that Frazier served. A Nonpartisan administration could be depended upon to go to any lengths to make the Bank succeed. Their reputation with the farmers depended upon its success. On the other hand the Bank of North Dakota was anathema to the I. V. A. political organization. To " turn the key in the door " of the Bank was the cause to which many an I. V. A. leader pledged himself with the fervor of a crusader. So even if Governor Nestos personally might have felt some sympathy toward a state-owned bank, he was in no position to manifest it for he was the servant of a political organization that would tolerate no compromise on the question of the state industrial program. The wonder is that bolder schemes designed to put the Bank out of business were not attempted. The probable explanation is that memory of the defeat of the I. V. A. sponsored Rural Credit Law remained a warning to the Independent Administration that the voters wanted to see the Bank given a fair trial.

However, if the key could not be safely turned in the door of the Bank openly, the same end could be accomplished covertly by making the Bank impotent. All that it required was to prevent the sale of bonds,[1] slow down the operations of the farm-loan department, devitalize other activities of the Bank and show that it was operating at a loss.

[1] When the Independent Industrial Commisssion came into office they threatened to bring suit to test the validity of the contract entered into by the Nonpartisan Industrial Commission and Spitzer, Rorick & Co. upon the eve of the former's retirement. Thereupon the contract was modified so that only $1,100,000 mill and elevator bonds and $3,000,000 real estate bonds should be delivered on the terms of the old contract, and Spitzer, Rorick & Co. agreed to take $400,000 Bank bonds bearing five per cent. Aside from these the only other bonds sold in 1922 were $600,000 mill and elevator bonds. These were sold on June 30, to the Minnesota Loan and Trust Company of Minneapolis at a very favorable premium.

Then, perchance, the farmers themselves would come to believe that the Bank was worthless and would rise up and demand its liquidation. Thus the odious State Bank could be made to condemn itself, and the administration that "turned the key in [its] door" would be commended by even the farmers for having moved in the direction of economy and efficiency.

CONCLUSIONS

A year and a half of operation reveals little to support the view that the Bank, under the Independent Administration, can ever become a vital force in solving the farm credit problem in North Dakota. A Nonpartisan institution can be of little service when operated by members of the I. V. A. Politics are far too acrimonious in North Dakota to expect that. If Governor Nestos was sincere in making his campaign promises and in what he said in his inaugural address, then, apparently, his political advisers lost little time in telling him in no uncertain manner that the successful operation of the Bank of North Dakota was no part of the plan or policy of the I. V. A. The result is that the Bank has given little support to agriculture. The present administration would probably be the first to admit that the Bank's performance is unsatisfactory.

CHAPTER VIII

CONCLUSIONS

During the first half of 1923 the operation of the Bank followed the lines laid down in 1922. Nothing had developed to warrant any change in the conclusions thus far arrived at. Therefore, this last chapter may be devoted to a general criticism of the institution. From time to time throughout this monograph opportunity has been taken to criticize various points of weakness in the Bank Act and in the policy adopted by the Bank officials. Now an attempt will be made to appraise the fundamental structure of the institution. At the risk of some repetition, it is proposed to analyze five main principles upon which its founders built. Thereafter recommendations will be made as to what appear to be the most necessary changes in the laws governing the Bank.

THE FIRST PRINCIPLE

The first of the five principles might perhaps more properly be called a tenet. But the belief that existing banking systems were utterly inadequate was so deep-rooted that there will be little exaggeration if this belief is listed among the principles upon which the Bank was reared. The founders were convinced that the Bank which they were creating was sorely needed and that it could in no wise be superfluous. Were they correct in this conviction?

There is an important minority in North Dakota who believe that there was no field for the Bank and that the state was being adequately served by the existing banking systems. But the majority, no doubt, hold that the existing agencies by no means met the credit requirements. During the past few years there has been a tremendous clamor for new and better banking machinery. Farmers demanded more and cheaper loans. Such agitation, however, must not be permitted to confuse sound judgment. The fact that an important group in North Dakota clamored for money is not necessarily proof positive that a legitimate satisfaction was being denied them. Long ago Adam Smith observed the perennial agitation for more and cheaper funds and commented upon it as follows:

> No complaint, however, is more common than that of a scarcity of money. Money, like wine, must always be scarce with those who have neither wherewithal to buy it, nor credit to borrow it. Those who have either, will seldom be in want either of the money or of the wine which they have occasion for. This complaint, however, of the scarcity of money, is not always confined to improvident spendthrifts. It is sometimes general through a whole mercantile town, and the country in its neighborhood. Over-trading is the common cause of it. Sober men, whose projects have been disproportioned to their capitals, are as likely to have neither wherewithal to buy money, nor credit to borrow it, as prodigals whose expense has been disproportioned to their revenue. Before their projects can be brought to bear, their stock is gone, and their credit with it. They run about everywhere to borrow money, and everybody tells them that they have none to lend.

These observations of a century and a half ago still meet with the approval of many people. Not a few in North Dakota believe that the financial distress of the farmers is the result of improvidence or poor business judgment, and conclude that nothing can be gained by trying to provide more and cheaper credit.

[1] *Wealth of Nations* (McCulloch's ed.). p. 191.

But there are certain facts that attest the need of better banking facilities in North Dakota than individual enterprise had afforded. It will be recalled that in Chapter I some figures were given which showed that North Dakota farmers were compelled to pay inordinately high interest rates on both long and short time loans. It was shown that even by paying these exorbitant rates they could not always secure from local institutions the banking service that the farmers' economic position, in their judgment, warranted. Surely few will deny that such circumstances indicate the lack of proper banking facilities.

But will not the banks provided for by the Federal Farm Loan Act now amply supply credit needs? Apparently not. Thus far only one joint-stock land bank has been chartered to operate in North Dakota and it operates only in fourteen of the fifty-three counties.[1] The Federal Land Bank of St. Paul has done notable work in the state, but even it has its limitations.[2] These have been candidly pointed out by its president, Mr. E. G. Quamme. His statement should silence those who have maintained that the Bank of North Dakota was superfluous and could only be an expense to the taxpayers of the state. In 1919, before the Bank of North Dakota was organized, consequently before it became a political tool, President Quamme of the Federal Land Bank of St. Paul recognized the need for an auxiliary institution in the following words: [3]

North Dakota needs a rural credits system. There are lots of farmers in the state that we can't reach for one reason or another. . . . For instance, the federal land bank doesn't lend money on unimproved land. The farm must be a going con-

[1] See Appendix B.

[2] See Appendix A.

[3] As reported in the *Fargo Courier-News*, May 9, 1919.

cern before we are permitted to make a loan. That is the place for the state to step in. North Dakota needs that sort of rural credits to help these men get on their feet. When they have got on their feet, and a farm, as we consider farms in the federal land bank system, established, they can obtain a loan thru our system and release the state's money for another man who is just beginning to establish a farm.

It appears, therefore, that the founders' convictions regarding the need for a bank are currently supported both by appearance and by official opinion.

THE SECOND PRINCIPLE

The second principle was that the new banking machinery should take the form of a State Bank and that public money should be an important factor in its operation.

It was this principle that suffered the most violent criticism at the hands of the Bank's opponents. Because of it they anathematized the Bank as a thing obnoxious. All the exaggerated fear of socialism that has developed since the war was capitalized against the institution, and whether reasonable or not, it proved to be a tremendous deterrent to progress.

To be sure there are plenty of people whose maturity of intellect enables them to resist the impulse to yield to hysteria whenever the word socialism is breathed, who, nevertheless, are utterly opposed to government ownership of business enterprises. They have been reared in a tradition of more than a century and a half which teaches that individual initiative and enterprise will suffice to produce the commodities and services required by the public. They fear the inefficiency and infidelity with which many public offices have been administered. They advocate, instead, that some sort of cooperative enterprise be resorted to. Such schemes enjoy no little popularity. It is coming to be a universal opinion that most of the farmers' problems involving financing, buying and selling can best be solved by some sort of cooperative effort.

The logic of those who favor cooperation, but have an aversion for state enterprise may be challenged. It appears especially faulty when the problems of the North Dakota farmers are being considered. In a state where eighty to eighty-five per cent of the population are engaged in the same business, cooperative enterprise and state enterprise are at bottom the same thing. For the state is but the collective body of individuals cooperating in the attainment of certain desirable ends that can be got more advantageously by combined action than by individual effort. The scope of state action has never been definitely limited to the attainment of special desiderata. It varies with time and place. Its extension is one of the remarkable economic developments of modern times. State action has gained in popularity and momentum from generation to generation.

A grave danger in supplanting private with government enterprise is that the latter is likely to be premature. This is especially dangerous in countries where public office is still too often looked upon as a sinecure at the disposal of political leaders, or as a powerful engine to gain advantage in private pursuits. Cooperation on a scale as magnificent as state enterprise calls for a fine sense of public honor and a true appreciation of public responsibility on the part of office-holders. It further requires that every precaution be taken to remove the temptations to use the enterprise or office for personal and political advantage.

On the whole it may be said that there was some reason for creating a State Bank in North Dakota. Had the management been surrounded by even ordinary safeguards against political cupidity and attack, the Bank might well have been directed in the interest of the citizens. The founders might then have been well-advised in adhering to the principle of state ownership.

THE THIRD PRINCIPLE

In a previous chapter it was pointed out that the Bank of North Dakota was designed to be a central reserve bank in which the state banks could concentrate their reserves. It was thought that the "entire financial worth" of the state would thus be mobilized to best advantage.

Central reserve banking has enjoyed a considerable success in a number of countries. It has usually resulted in a more economical use of the country's currency and in a greater mobility of bank reserves. From these two primary results others have sprung. Thus all the benefits accruing to the local banks, and through them to the business public, which arise from the privileges of rediscounting and borrowing, of maintaining smaller reserves and of better exchange facilities, may well be ascribed to the central reserve system.

However, it is doubtful whether the North Dakota credit problem was brought much nearer solution through the application of the central reserve banking principle to the State Bank. Some minor benefits would, indeed, result. But the principal advantage to the state would be lost because of its peculiar industrial nature. North Dakota has but one main industry and the seasonal credit requirements are the same throughout the state. A central bank could not transfer funds to one section of the state in need of them for moving crops without depriving another section of money which it needed for the same purpose. At such times funds must be drawn from without the state. Hence it is difficult to see how much could be gained through the application of the central reserve principle to the Bank of North Dakota.

THE FOURTH PRINCIPLE

The fusion of mortgage banking with reserve banking represents a fourth principle upon which the Bank was established. This was one of the most ill-advised concepts that entered into the Bank's structure. The two types of banking have few things in common and they differ greatly in their most vital requirements.

The mortgage bank has little interest in deposits. It seeks funds that are awaiting permanent investment. Its loans are made on collateral that is not easy to convert into cash on short notice without suffering substantial loss.

On the other hand, a reserve bank depends almost entirely on deposits for its working funds. Moreover, because these deposits represent bank reserves they are subject to withdrawal at any time. Hence it is exceedingly important that a reserve bank should keep on hand at all times a large percentage of its deposits. Federal reserve banks are required by law to keep at least thirty-five per cent of their deposits in gold or lawful money. Furthermore, such investments as a reserve bank makes must be in paper that is quick to mature and whose collateral is property that can be converted into cash with ease and without serious loss. Such paper is seldom to be found in a mortgage bank's portfolio.

It will be seen, therefore, that the two types of banks demand very different policies and management. To endeavor to fuse them is to invite disaster. The Bank of North Dakota suffered great embarrassment because it attempted to weld into one these fundamentally different businesses.

THE FIFTH PRINCIPLE

The control of the Bank was vested in a body composed of state officials. This meant that its destiny was largely in the hands of a group who held their offices by virtue of popular political election. At first sight this appears to afford a valuable check and control over the management, for they are then directly answerable to the people. Their stewardship of the public institution must recommend itself to the citizens or the officials will suffer defeat in the elections;—that, at least, is the theory.

But how does practice work out? It has proved that, just because its office is so dependent upon public approval and favor, the controlling body comes to be concerned more with political maneuvering than with the fearless operation of the institution along lines known to be sound. It has proved that instead of serving as an impetus to excellent public service, the fear of recall or of failure at the polls tempts officials to manipulate their posts for the purpose of gaining personal political advantage; and this, it must be confessed, does not usually coincide with the public's interest. Both administrations left much to be desired in the management of the Bank of North Dakota. Its history abounds with illustrations of political manipulation. Perhaps no other single factor has so weakened the Bank's position; and reform of necessity will commence with a complete change in the status of its officials. The North Dakota experiment should serve as a warning to those who believe that the officers of a public enterprise will serve the community best if they are constantly harassed by political adversaries. The truth is that such officers must be free from political attack; otherwise they have no mind to devote to the public interest. Their public trust is of necessity subverted into a private political weapon.

The history of the Commonwealth Bank of Australia is illuminating on this point. By the Commonwealth Bank Act of 1911-20 the Australians created a bank which in many ways is similar to the Bank of North Dakota. It is owned entirely by the Commonwealth, has no share capital, acts as fiscal agent for the government, enjoys the government's guarantee of its obligations, and in many other ways parallels the North Dakota Institution. It began operations in 1913 and from the beginning has enjoyed the confidence of the citizens and has rendered conspicuous banking service. It is generally considered to be a highly successful institution and the growth of its business has been remarkable. Every development indicates that the Commonwealth Bank of Australia enjoys first-class management. How is that secured?

A very great amount of power is vested in the governor of the bank, who is appointed by the government and holds office for seven years. This arrangement frees him from the necessity of using the bank as a political weapon. He is free to operate the bank as his business judgment, and not his political judgment, dictates. Whether or not he will do so depends upon the individual chosen to fill the office. The chief obstruction to sound management, which would embarrass any governor, is cleared away, and unbiased management is possible and feasible. It may be that the day will come when Australians will see the need for encroaching on the autocratic powers of the governor of the bank and for making the bank act more specific in certain details. But the provisions for the appointment of the governor and for his term of office will without doubt continue to justify themselves. The Commonwealth was fortunate in the selection of Mr. Denison Miller for the governorship. At the time of his appointment, Mr. Miller was metropolitan supervisor of the Bank of New Zealand. He differed in his political views with the government that appointed him, but he was an experienced banker. The development of the bank evidences the wisdom of the selection. However, even a man of Mr. Miller's ability and integrity would likely have made a very mediocre showing without the shelter from political attack that a seven-year appointment afforded him.

The lesson for North Dakota is clear. The state can never expect its Bank to enjoy even mediocre success until it in some way shelters its officials from constant political attack. How this may be accomplished will be enlarged upon below.

GENERAL CONCLUSIONS

The gravest mistake that the legislators who drafted the Bank Act made was to leave so many vital decisions of policy to a politically elective body. It is difficult to see how the Bank of North Dakota can ever be of much service to the state so long as it continues to be used as a lever to gain political advantage for its officials. The first prerequisite to successful operation is to free the Bank from political control.

To accomplish this end two changes appear necessary. The first and most important is to revise the Bank Act so that administrative officers cannot so readily pervert the original intention of the law, and use it to further their own political ends. For instance, Section 14 which empowers the Industrial Commission to select the depositary banks and to determine the terms and conditions under which redeposits of public funds will be made must be revised in the interest of the Bank's future solvency. In a previous chapter it was pointed out that the power conferred on the Industrial Commission by Section 14 was not always wisely used and therefore led to some unfortunate situations. There is no good reason why the terms and conditions of redeposit cannot be established in the Bank Act. If they were, it is safe to assume that public deposits could never be rushed into failing banks, but would of necessity be placed in the strongest and most solvent banks available.

The same criticism applies to Section 15. This section

empowers the Industrial Commission to determine the terms, rules and regulations under which the Bank may loan funds to "counties, cities, or political subdivisions of the State, or to state or national banks." Here again experience has shown that this power over loans and advances was abused. Officials of a public bank are sure to be beset by those who desire accommodation on a political basis, and they suffer endless criticism because of alleged favoritism in granting loans. Such being the case, it is difficult indeed for bank officials to conduct their operations on an impartial and business-like basis. But if the law were changed so as to establish definite rules and standards of loan-making to which bank officials were compelled to conform, then there would result this double gain; untrustworthy officials would be restrained from abusing their power of loaning public funds, and honest and sincere public servants would enjoy some protection against unscrupulous politicians who constantly harass them and make honest and efficient management virtually impossible.

These two examples do not exhaust the possibilities for improvement of the Bank Act by transforming general provisions which leave vital questions of policy to the discretion of the Industrial Commission into specific provisions demanding definite standards and requiring sound practice. They are, however, sufficient to show what can and should be done.

The second change that suggests itself is that the control of the Bank should be vested in a body other than the Industrial Commission. It is impossible to believe that the Bank's operations can be divorced from politics so long as the Bank is under its control. The three members of the Industrial Commission hold their office by virtue of popular political election to other state offices. Not only is their regular term of office short, but they are subject to recall at any time during their term. Is it surprising that men whose tenure of office is so very dependent on popular favor would use this Bank which they direct, either to discredit their political opponents, or to curry favor with their political friends? Neither administration was able to resist the temptation to manipulate the Bank for political advantages.[1] The law must be changed in this respect. Legal provision should be made whereby a board of three members would be appointed by the governor with the "advice and consent" of the legislature. In order to get a representative board the usual precautions respecting political affiliations should be taken. At least one member should be a man actively engaged in farming; at least one should be a man of practical banking experience. The members of this board should, when appointed, hold office for not less than four and preferably six years. There would be an advantage in appointing the first three members for terms of two, four and six years respectively. Thus every two years a vacancy would occur and the board would enjoy a greater degree of stability and continuity than would otherwise be possible. Thus might well be removed the greatest obstacle that the Bank has had to overcome. The Bank's reverses were not chiefly due to bad crops or bad prices or even primarily bad management. Bad politics were, in last

[1] The most open use of the Bank to gain political advantage under the I. V. A. Administration that has come to the author's attention was in the refusal of the Industrial Commission to make good their promise of a $140,000 loan to the Equity Packing Company of Fargo. According to the *Fargo Courier-News*, June 6, 8, 14, 16 and July 4, 1922, Mr. Theo. Nelson, Secretary of the I. V. A., told President Reichert of the Equity that he was instructed to take care of "the political end of the loan". This political end seems to have been that John L. Middlethun, one of the board of directors, a Nonpartisan and candidate for the state senate, withdraw from the race. President Reichert refused this demand and the loan was refused. The Equity lost heavily through subsequent foreclosure proceedings.

analysis, the main incumbrance of the Bank. Making those who are directly responsible for its control free from political attack, and providing for their selection in such manner as to insure a reasonable balance between liberal and conservative, would, it is believed, go far toward restoring to great usefulness an institution which has suffered at the hands of popularly elected officials.

Having purged the Bank of the political evil the legislators should next address themselves to the task of definitely separating the farm-loan department from the rest of the Bank. The Independent Administration has made a good beginning in segregating the farm-loan business. Legal provision should be made to insure its permanent separation.

Finally those who will have opportunity to mould the Bank's future should carefully consider the reasonable functions of a State Bank and determine what it may legitimately do to aid its citizens in their business. If this is done it will be seen that little is gained by centralizing the reserves of the state banks, or even by endeavoring to draw the public funds into one central reservoir. North Dakota is too new a state to be able to get on with her own capital. Like every other new community she must rely chiefly upon outside funds. Such being the case it is vain to vilify the capitalists of money centers. They cannot be coerced into loaning their funds on what they consider insufficient security. The capitalist is the most cautious and conservative of business men. To him a return of four per cent on an investment made close at home or through machinery and in securities with which he is thoroughly familiar seems more desirable than an eight per cent return on an investment one or two thousand miles away, the security for which he has never seen and the earning power of which has never been thoroughly established. The capitalist is an eager purchaser of what he considers good securities. Let him be convinced that a note or a mortgage is first class security and, other things being equal, a fraction of a per cent is sufficient difference in the return to influence his purchase. This well-known truth must be borne in mind by those who attempt to improve the position of the rural borrower. Their foremost purpose should be to make attractive the loans that are offered to the investor. They should seek to embody in farm debentures all the features that attract conservative investors to other types of securities. This gives the clue to the proper function of the State Bank. It is to guarantee the credit of the citizens. If it, being on the field, knows a loan to be safe—so safe that it is willing to make it—then it will be of inestimable worth to the farmers of the state if to their individual credit be added the faith and credit of the state in which they reside. For, with such security, it is possible to go before the most conservative investors in the capital markets of the world and compete to advantage for the cheap funds there obtainable on high grade securities.

The Bank of North Dakota's principal function, then, should be to guarantee the credit of the farmers. This is a legitimate function of a cooperative institution and one to which much of the success enjoyed by them may be ascribed The individual farmer's credit weakness lies in his isolated position, and in the lack of ready security acceptable to money-lenders. In cooperative combination the farmer finds credit strength. The money-lender is willing to advance funds on reasonable terms if the individual farmer's credit is backed up by that of his neighbors and thus guaranteed by the community. This principle is imbedded in our Federal Land Bank System, it is the backbone of many of the European rural credit systems, and it is found in some sections of the act creating the Bank of North Dakota. Had the North Dakota Institution adhered steadfastly to this one function most of its embarrassment because of the freezing of public funds in farm loans could not have arisen.

The same principle can and should be applied in making short-time loans. There are far fewer precedents for it in this field than in the mortgage banking business. Still there are many good reasons for believing that it would be successful. The Bank of North Dakota might secure a large amount of money for the farmers at relatively cheap rates if it would sell short-time notes secured by commodity paper and guaranteed by the state. There is good reason to believe that three to six months notes secured by warehouse receipts for wheat and guaranteed by the state of North Dakota would sell at favorable prices. Thus the Bank would be of great service in bringing to the state the capital which its business so greatly requires. To guarantee the credit of the farmers so that capitalists will make them loans on favorable terms is all that the Bank of North Dakota can and should legitimately do.

Doubtless such a bank will continue to be opposed by some local bankers and loan-sharks who are preying upon the loan-seeking farmers. It will mean, of course, that the quasi-monopoly which they enjoy will be destroyed. However, the local banker has little to fear. Prosperity of the community in which he does business cannot work hardship on him. Indeed it would have the opposite effect. He should rejoice in the presence of any institution that can aid in lifting his debt-ridden community to a state of prosperity. No such solace can be offered the loan-shark, and no one will mourn his disappearance.

It is to be hoped that the legislators will carefully revise the Bank Act so as to remedy some of the obvious defects that now exist, and that the Bank officials will increasingly recognize their public duty and responsibility. The farmers of North Dakota have an institution which, if properly reorganized and operated, can increase their credit standing so as to save them large sums in their annual interest bill. The Bank is a cooperative enterprise on an extended scale. It calls for an equally pronounced spirit of cooperation and citizenship. Given this, it may well become one of the means of bringing prosperity and progress to North Dakota.

APPENDIX A[1]

Federal Land Bank Activities in North Dakota

In accordance with the Federal Farm Loan Act the Federal Farm Loan Board was organized August 7, 1916. On March 1, 1917 the first charter was granted to a federal land bank; and on March 27, 1917 the first charter was granted to a national farm-loan association.

North Dakota together with Minnesota, Wisconsin and Michigan comprises the Seventh Federal Farm Loan District. The Federal Land Bank of St. Paul operates in this district. The following table shows the growth of its business in North Dakota.

	National farm loan associations chartered	*Loans made*	*Total amount loaned*	*Average loan*
November 30, 1917	46	——	$1,825,600	——
November 30, 1918	155	3,685	10,324,300	$2,801
November 30, 1919	173	5,475	16,783,600	3,065
December 31, 1920	175	6,566	21,616,900	3,292
November 30, 1921	187	6,924	23,570,900	3,404
December 31, 1922	191	8,521	31,578,000	3,706
April 1, 1923	189	9,078	34,225,400	3,770

The following table gives a detailed summary of the work in North Dakota of the Federal Land Bank of St. Paul from the organization of the Bank to October 31, 1922.

[1] Appendix A is based on the first six annual reports of the Federal Farm Loan Board, and the tables were compiled from data taken from them and from correspondence with the Federal Land Bank of St. Paul.

Number of borrowers	7,778
Amount applied for	$30,859,895
Amount granted	$27,760,650
Total acres mortgaged	1,854,670
Appraised valuations:	
Land	$60,961,520
Buildings	$17,356,052
Total	$78,317,572

The amount of money loaned by federal land banks in the three states which have received the largest total loans from these banks is shown in the following table. From the beginning North Dakota has been among the three states enjoying this privilege.

		National farm loan associations chartered	*Loans made*	*Total amount loaned*	*Average loan*
	Kansas	81	——	$3,594,000	——
1917	North Dakota	46	——	1,825,600	——
	Washington	96	——	1,781,850	——
	Texas	280	5,250	13,568,461	2,584
1918	North Dakota	155	3,685	10,324,300	2,801
	Montana	122	2,934	7,321,790	2,495
	Texas	331	10,945	31,408,401	2,870
1919	Iowa	138	2,539	17,995,150	7,087
	North Dakota	173	5,475	16,783,600	3,065
	Texas	342	13,796	40,816,066	2,958
1920	Iowa	141	3,382	24,124,350	7,133
	North Dakota	175	6,566	21,616,900	3,292
	Texas	343	16,263	48,514,291	2,983
1921	Iowa	141	3,923	27,604,750	7,037
	North Dakota	187	6,924	23,570,900	3,404
	Texas	365	24,825	74,366,791	2,996
1922	Iowa	148	5,015	34,540,550	6,887
	North Dakota	191	8,521	31,578,000	3,706

APPENDIX B[1]

Joint Stock Land Bank Activities in North Dakota

The Federal Farm Loan Act of 1916 made provision whereby ten or more natural persons might form a corporation under federal charter to be known as a joint stock land bank, " for carrying on the business of lending on farm mortgage security and issuing farm loan bonds." These joint stock land banks are private institutions, and the government is not, as in the case of federal land banks, permitted to subscribe to the capital stock. However, they are supervised by the federal farm loan board, inspected twice yearly by its examiners, and their appraisals are under its control. While the amount of business that they may do is limited to a smaller percentage of their capital than is the case with federal land banks, yet in other ways they are less restricted. The amount that they may loan to an individual, the use to which the funds will be put, and the occupation of the borrower are not so restricted as in the case of federal land banks. Joint stock land banks are not permitted to charge more than six per cent interest. They may do business in the state in which their principal office is located and in one contiguous state.

To the present only one joint stock land bank has been chartered to operate in North Dakota. The Minneapolis Trust Joint Stock Land Bank of Minneapolis, Minnesota,

[1] Sources of information used in the preparation of this appendix are, the Federal Farm Loan Act, a folder furnished by the Minneapolis Trust Joint Stock Land Bank entitled "Minneapolis Trust Area in North Dakota", and correspondence with the above named bank.

chartered May 2, 1922 and may operate in both Minnesota and North Dakota.

The Minneapolis Trust Joint Stock Land Bank does not make loans throughout the entire state of North Dakota, but so far has confined its operations to fourteen counties lying in the Red River Valley. It is said that these fourteen counties constitute more than twenty-six per cent of the farming area of North Dakota. The fourteen counties are: Barnes, Cass, Cavalier, Grand Forks, Griggs, Nelson, Pembina, Ramsey, Ramson, Richland, Sargent, Steele, Traill, and Walsh. The following table shows the amount and nature of business done by the Minneapolis Trust Joint Stock Land Bank in its first year of operation.

Number of loans	540
Acres covered	140,628
Amount of loans	$3,249,100.00
Average size loan, about	$6,000.00
Average loan per acre	$23.10
Average value of land in area per acre (1919)	$68.60

APPENDIX C[1]

The War Finance Corporation and North Dakota

Originally created as a war agency, as its name implies, the War Finance Corporation was empowered by the Congress in March, 1919, to assist in the task of reconstruction and readjustment. It was authorized, in order to promote commerce with foreign nations through the extension of credits, and to aid in the transition from the conditions of war to the conditions of peace, to make advances not exceeding $1,000,000,000 to American exporters and American banking institutions for the purpose of financing the exportation of domestic products. This authority was exercised until May, 1920, when the activities of the Corporation were suspended.

In the autumn of 1920, when the collapse in commodity markets became acute, the question of our exports again became a matter of general interest; and the Congress, in January, 1921, adopted the following joint resolution directing the activities of the Corporation be resumed:

That the Secretary of the Treasury and the members of the War Finance Corporation are hereby directed to revive the activities of the War Finance Corporation, and that said Corporation be at once rehabilitated with the view of assisting in the financing of the exportation of agricultural and other products to foreign countries.

[1] This appendix is made up of various paragraphs and statements taken directly from the fourth and fifth annual reports of the War Finance Corporation. The last sentence in the appendix is the only exception. It is taken from correspondence with the War Finance Corporation under date of May 5, 1923.

In view of the terms of the resolution, the evident intent of Congress, and conditions throughout the country, the directors of the Corporation, in resuming operations, concentrated their efforts in the beginning largely on the development of methods for the financing of exports of agricultural commodities.

With the development of the activities of the Corporation, it was increasingly clear that export financing alone would not be sufficient to meet the needs of agriculture. On account of the changed situation in Europe and of the conditions existing in this country, we were confronted with the necessity of selling our staple agricultural products more gradually than in former years; and it became more and more apparent that provision must be made for the carrying of our commodities in larger quantities for a longer period of marketing.

Not only was the market abroad slow, but it was demonstrated, after careful inquiry, that our own merchants and manufacturers were operating on the basis of the lowest possible stocks, and were buying only to meet current demands. This naturally resulted in forcing large quantities of raw materials, which normally are carried by mills, wholesalers, jobbers, and retailers, back upon the original producers and the banks which do their financing. The producers were unable to market their products as rapidly as formerly, large numbers of them were unable to liquidate their loans, and an unusually heavy burden was imposed upon the local banking institutions, seriously straining their resources and facilities. A condition of acute distress developed in the agricultural sections of the country, and if disaster was to be averted extraordinary action was needed to meet the situation.

After a careful study of the whole problem, certain amendments to the War Finance Corporation act were proposed, considered by the Congress, and embodied in the agricultural credits act of August 24, 1921. The act broadened the powers of the Corporation, and gave it authority to make advances not only to exporters and banking institutions, but also to dealers in, and handlers of, agricultural products, including cooperative associations, for the purpose of financing the carrying of such products until they could be exported or sold for export in an orderly manner. Such advances may be made until July 1, 1922, for periods not exceeding one year, but the time for payment may, in the discretion of the Corporation, be extended for periods not exceeding three years from the dates upon which the advances were originally made.

The act also empowered the Corporation to make advances to "any bank, banker or trust company in the United States," or to cooperative associations of producers, which may have made advances for agricultural purposes, including the breeding, raising, fattening, and marketing of live stock, or may have discounted or rediscounted notes, drafts, bills of exchange or other negotiable instruments issued for such purposes. Such advances may be made for periods not exceeding one year, with discretion in the War Finance Corporation to renew them for periods not extending beyond three years from the dates on which the advances were originally made. In exceptional cases, the Corporation was authorized to purchase from domestic banks, bankers, or trust companies paper secured by agricultural products, including live stock; and it was further authorized to purchase, sell, or otherwise deal in acceptances, adequately secured, issued by Edge Law banking corporations, to assist them in promoting the exportation of agricultural and manufactured products.

The act provided that all advances shall be made upon promissory note or notes, or other instrument or instruments, in such form as to impose on the borrower a primary and unconditional obligation to repay the advance at maturity, with interest as stipulated therein, and shall be fully and adequately secured in each instance by indorsement, guaranty, pledge, or otherwise. The aggregate amount of advances made and paper purchased and outstanding at any one time was limited to $1,000,000,000, and the Corporation was authorized to issue its bonds to the extent of three times its capital stock, or $1,500,000,000.

The Corporation is not authorized under the law to deal directly with individual producers. It is reaching the farmer not only through cooperative associations but also through their local banking institutions.

Altogether, the corporation has authorized more than 6,600 loans to banking institutions for agricultural purposes. Of these, more than 5,500, or approximately 83 per cent, represent advances to State banks, and 1,100, or 17 per cent, to national banks. In terms of dollars, the loans to State banks, amounting to $135,430,000, constitute 80 per cent of the whole, and the loans to national banks, totaling $32,828,000, 20 per cent. Thus the corporation has provided during the emergency a rediscount facility especially needed by banks in the country districts not members of the Federal reserve system, enabling them to meet the agricultural needs of their communities in a way that otherwise would not have been possible.

A special feature of the work of the War Finance Corporation during the past year was the financing of cooperative marketing associations.

During the current season the corporation has approved loans totaling $114,000,000 to 24 cooperative marketing associations in 18 States to assist in the orderly marketing of 1922 crops.

During the season of 1921-22 the corporation authorized

loans totaling $64,000,000 to 19 cooperative marketing associations in 15 States to assist in the orderly marketing of the products of their members. Of this amount, only $19,198,000 was actually called for by the associations, although the entire amount was available to them. It developed as the season progressed that the local banks were able and willing to take care of their needs to a greater extent than had been anticipated.

The Corporation has actually advanced $20,729,685.16 to banking institutions and cooperative associations of producers in the State of North Dakota, under Section 24 of the Act.

INDEX

Bei Fragen zur Produktsicherheit wenden Sie sich bitte an:
If you have any questions regarding product safety,
please contact:

Walter de Gruyter GmbH
Genthiner Straße 13
10785 Berlin
productsafety@degruyterbrill.com